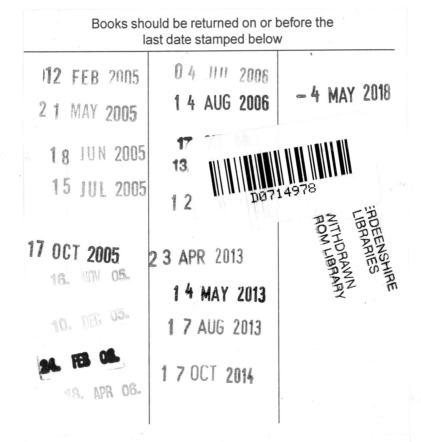
**ABERDEENSHIRE LIBRARY
AND INFORMATION SERVICE**

MELD Magill, Richard UM

Start to sign! /
Richard Magill,
Anne Hodgson
                    371.
                        912
1566195

RNID

Published by

RNID, 19-23 Featherstone Street, London EC1Y 8SL

© RNID 2000

First published 2000
Second edition 2001
Third edition 2003

ISBN 0 900634 73 1 paperback 1st edition
ISBN 0 900634 84 7 paperback 2nd edition
ISBN 1 904296 02 5 paperback 3rd edition

The handshape illustrations used in this publication are reproduced with
the permission of the Deaf Studies Research Unit, University of Durham.
The handshape illustrations are taken from the *Dictionary of British Sign
Language/English* (Faber and Faber, 1992). The dictionary was
produced by the Deaf Studies Research Unit for the British Deaf
Association.

Contents

Acknowledgements

This book would not have been possible without the involvement of many people.

The models were RNID staff: Celal Djemal, Helen Ellis, Roz German, Barbara Laumets, Angela Miller, Asha Nauth, Sara Olsen, Sally Paull, Siân Smith and Rebecca Tadman.

Particular thanks go to Sally Paull and Linda Richards who made time in their busy schedules to comment on the text at different stages. Thanks also go to Robert Farquharson, Rosanna Preston, Bob Wray, Susannah Calderan, Kathryn Merritt, Stefanie Hafner and the interpreters who supported us.

RNID's Publications Team looked after the project as a whole: Julie Goldsmith, Yael Hodder and Suzanne Mullins were the designers, Lynn Jackson was editor, and Bridget Middleton, Philippa Smart and Paul Strange were project managers.

Jens Storch was our photographer and Jennie Dooge was responsible for the layout.

Thanks also go to David Brien of the University of Durham for many helpful suggestions and to Clive Mason for the foreword.

Foreword by Clive Mason

As a user of British Sign Language, I am delighted to see this latest edition of *Start to Sign!* More people start learning to sign every year and this book aims to help and encourage anyone who is taking sign language classes by reinforcing what you will learn, and providing a source of reference.

Many people start learning to sign for their own interest. Others learn because they know someone who is deaf, or because they have contact with deaf people at work. In addition to covering much of the vocabulary you need for everyday conversations, the book provides basic information about the grammar of BSL. BSL is not a translation of English – in fact there are signs that are very difficult to express in English at all – but a language in its own right, the language of the Deaf Community in Britain. Through BSL you will have the opportunity to learn about the Deaf Community and experience the richness and variety of Deaf Culture.

Clive Mason is an active member of the Deaf Community who campaigns for Deaf rights. His love of language led him to work in the media field, and he presented the BBC's See Hear programme for many years, after which he lectured at Wolverhampton University. He spent some time with Independent Media Support Limited, providing in-vision-signing access on Digital TV, before taking on the role of Course Director for the innovative Sign Media course at City University. Clive also works as a freelance media consultant.

7

We are delighted to be reprinting *Start to sign!*

As we go to our third edition we are pleased to see that *Start to sign!* continues to be a valuable and popular resource for students new to BSL. Although the basic text remains the same we have made a few minor corrections which help make this latest edition even easier to follow.

We would like to thank everyone who has kindly taken time to suggest helpful changes.

In March 2003, after many years of campaigning, the government officially recognised BSL as a language in its own right. This is a major development which paves the way for greater opportunities for deaf people in the UK. This includes the right for deaf children to be taught in BSL, the training of BSL tutors and BSL/English interpreters, recognition of BSL as a valid academic qualification and a greater use of BSL across society.

Introduction to British Sign Language

History

We can probably assume that sign language has been around for as long as there have been deaf people who wanted to communicate. First records of British Sign Language (BSL) date from the 16th century; there are even earlier records of sign language in other countries. BSL was used in schools for deaf children and learned by increasing numbers of people until the end of the last century. Then in 1880, at a conference in Milan, a group of teachers working with deaf children – who believed the teaching of sign language was detrimental to the acquisition of spoken language – voted that sign language should no longer be taught in schools. This decision affected several European countries. In England it meant that only spoken and written English were taught, and that use of BSL in schools was actively discouraged. This 'Oral Method' remained dominant for almost 100 years. However, in 1979, Conrad's book *The Deaf School Child* revealed that profoundly deaf children were leaving school at 16 with an average reading age of less than nine. From this time, attitudes towards the use of BSL with deaf children in schools began to change and become more positive.

Over the last 20 years, BSL has gained a great deal in popularity and influence. It is frequently seen on television, both when programmes use sign language interpreters to give sign language users access to them, and in programmes that are specifically targeted at deaf people. An increase in the numbers of Deaf people training as BSL tutors has led to the establishment of BSL classes all over the UK. More and more people are learning to sign and over 100,000 people have passed their Stage I (Basic) examination in BSL.

BSL today

How many people use BSL today? It is hard to be sure for two reasons:

Firstly, BSL is the language of the British Deaf Community. It is used by many people who are born deaf and learn to sign as children, BSL being their first language. However, only one deaf child in 10 has deaf parents, so there are many deaf people who learn BSL as their second language, after having learnt English. Some of these people describe BSL as their *preferred* language. Lots of deaf children learn BSL at school.

Secondly, some deaf people do not use BSL, but Sign Supported English, or SSE. SSE is not a language in its own right, independent of English, but more a kind of English with signs. Many people you see signing may be using SSE. Other people use neither BSL nor SSE, but elements of each, so that their signing is somewhere between the two. For this reason it is hard to give an exact figure for the number of sign language users. It is thought that, of the 9 million people in the UK with some degree of hearing loss, about 50,000 sign.

The Deaf Community and Deaf Culture

BSL users are also members of the Deaf Community. They describe themselves as Deaf, written with a capital 'D' to emphasise their Deaf identity, take part in Deaf events, and may attend Deaf Clubs and groups. Deaf people believe strongly in their right to participate fully and equally in society.

How to learn BSL and find classes

Nobody can learn BSL just from a book, or even from a video or CD-ROM. These are useful back-up resources if you want to remind yourself of signs, or practise at home, but the only way to learn BSL is from a Deaf person, ideally from a qualified BSL tutor.

Qualifications in BSL are at five levels; the first level is called Stage I. Curricula and examinations are set by the Council for the Advancement of Communication with Deaf People (CACDP). CACDP's address is on page 212. CACDP has a Tutor Policy, which sets out the recommended standards for BSL tutors. If you want to learn BSL and have not already found a sign language class, you can get details of courses in your area from the RNID Information Line, details are on page 211.

Popular myths

There are many misconceptions about sign language.

Sign language is not international; BSL is used only in Britain. Each country has its own sign language, although some sign languages are closely related to one another. American Sign Language and French Sign Language share similar roots, although they are now separate languages. Auslan (Australian Sign Language) and BSL are very similar.

BSL is not an 'invented' language, such as Esperanto. It evolved naturally as languages do. Like any language it has its own grammar and syntax. It can express anything that its users want to say and if there is no sign to express a particular idea, BSL users will develop one, in the same way that speakers of English form new words to describe new concepts. Examples of new signs in BSL are the signs for *Internet* and *e-mail*. Both *Internet* and *e-mail* are new words in English too.

It is very important to remember that, since BSL is a language in its own right, you cannot translate English into BSL, word for sign. Some English words or phrases have no direct translation into BSL, and some signs have no direct translation into English. As you learn more BSL you will understand the meanings of signs used from the context in which you see them, rather than by associating them with any English word. Examples of signs that are particularly difficult to put into English are multi-channel signs. There is more information about these on page 16.

Regional variation

Like spoken languages, BSL has many regional variations. For example, we show a numbering system on pages 207-210, but it is very possible that you will learn a different system at your BSL class. Colours are another group of signs with many regional variants. If you move about then it is useful to learn and remember different regional signs. You may find that the signs you learn are not always the same as the ones in this book. If you move from one part of the country to another, you may find that some of your signs have different meanings, or that you learn a second sign for something.

Left-handed people

The photographs in this book are of right-handed signing. If you are left-handed, you should use your left hand where our photographs show someone signing with their right hand. Where they use their left hand, you should use your right hand. Movements from one side to the other should be made in the opposite direction to that shown in the photographs. When you read the section on time lines, remember that the information we have given is for right-handed people, and that if you are left-handed you should place the time lines on the opposite side of your body.

The components of the language

Until they watch it closely, or begin to learn it themselves, most people think that BSL is just a series of gestures. In fact, it is far more complex than that. We can identify four basic components:

Handshape: how you hold your fingers and thumbs.

Movement: of your hand through a defined space.

Non-manual
features (NMFs):   facial expression and shoulder movement.

Spatial orientation: the relationship of the hand to the signer's body.

Structure

In English, a sentence is controlled by the verb; other parts of the sentence are organised in relation to it. The meaning of the sentence is often dependent on the position of other words in relation to the verb.

BSL is structured in a completely different way, and to learn it you must disregard what you know about English grammar because it is not relevant. In BSL, the first thing you sign in any utterance is usually the main subject, or topic. After that you define the subject by commenting on it. The sentence 'What is your name?' in English would therefore appear in BSL as:

you	→	name	→	what?
		lipshape		(questioning expression)

This structure, which is completely unlike the structure of English, is used by some spoken languages too.

Directional verbs

One feature of BSL is that some of its verbs can change direction. We have indicated these *directional verbs* throughout this book by putting **DV** under the photographs, but the pictures below give an example of how one of these verbs works. You can use the sign 'ask' by moving your hand from a position near to yourself towards someone to mean '*I* ask *you*' or '*I* am asking *you*'. If you use the same sign but begin it with your hand about 40 cm away and move it towards yourself that means '*you* are asking *me*' or '*you* ask *me*'. You can use the same sign to mean '*he/she/you/they* ask(s) *you/him/her/them*' by moving your hand from one 'person' or group of people in the defined signing space in front of you, to another.

I am asking you

Modification

Signs modify to add meaning. The three photographs below all use the sign for *raining*. NMFs – and in real life, how much you stress the signs – all show how heavy the rain is.

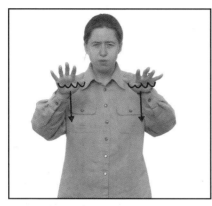

Light rain or drizzle

Heavier rain

Pouring with rain

The signing space

BSL users sign in a clearly defined space, which starts a little below waist level and goes up to a few centimetres above their head. It stretches to arm's length in front of them. The use of this space is extremely important to the meaning of what is signed.

Placement

Someone using BSL to describe something they have seen will situate all the components within the space in front of them at elbow height. They will first define the area – for example a room, field or road – and will then place items or actions inside that space, in precise relation to the confines of the space and what they are describing, as they visualise it, not as a mirror image. They may use their gaze to emphasise the placement of components within the space.

Iconicity

Some signs seem to look like the idea they represent. For example, if you look at the photograph of the sign for 'crab' on page 23, you can see it looks like a crab. The sign for 'sew' looks like someone sewing. This feature is called 'iconicity' or 'visual motivation'. These signs are not miming; they work within the grammar of BSL and conform to its rules. Many signs have this visual connection with their meaning – and many do not.

Time lines

Time is positioned around the body of the signer by means of one of four time lines:

- To our right, between waist and shoulder level, is a time line that indicates age, usually of children.

- A time line over the right shoulder indicates time on a large and general scale, from recently to years ago (see page 196 for 'long ago' and page 198 for 'recently').

- A time line along the left arm and hand shows precise time, measured in weeks.

- A time line that runs in front of you from left to right at elbow level shows continuous time.

Compound signs

Sometimes two signs together are used to make another meaning. Examples of these are 'decide' (page 181) and 'believe' (page 182).

Multi-channel signs

Multi-channel signs cannot easily be translated into English. They use more than one channel, for example a sign, movement and specific NMFs. They rarely have a direct equivalent in English and often it takes a whole phrase or more to capture the meaning of a multi-channel sign in English. Below is one example of a multi-channel sign, meaning 'I am not bothered'.

Lip patterns

Never forget that lip patterns are a very important part of BSL. The pictures for 'aunt', 'uncle', 'niece' and 'nephew' on page 105 illustrate this. The handshape and movement are the same for all four signs, but the lip pattern is different in each case.

Sign names

Deaf sign language users are often given sign names. Your BSL teacher will probably give you one. There are different kinds of sign names, for example a sign that shows:

- A physical feature of the person – such as a hairstyle.

- A characteristic, such as being fidgety or having a quick temper.

- A translation or pun on the person's English first name or surname, such as Dawn, Penny or Rose, Brown, Forest or Walker.

Some people fingerspell their initials, particularly if their first and second names begin with the same letter. For example, Sam Smith would be SS. People with a short first name such as Mel, Rob or Pam may just fingerspell it.

Here are some examples of sign names:

Richard was given his sign name at school. He was at school in Yorkshire where the sign for 11 is the sign shown in the second picture. Richard's name was number 11 on the register and he also had a habit of rubbing his nose. His sign name, shown in the first picture is a combination of these two things.

Sally's sign name is her initials, SP, fingerspelled. There is more information about fingerspelling below.

Rebecca's sign name is a mannerism; she pushes her hair behind her ears.

Fingerspelling

All letters of the English alphabet can be spelled on your hands. This alphabet – the manual alphabet or fingerspelling – is used to spell out the names of people or places that do not have sign names.

Some signs are developed from fingerspelling. For example, in parts of Britain, fingerspelled letters are used for days of the week. M spelled twice quickly is Monday, T twice is Tuesday, W twice is Wednesday; for Thursday spell Th once. Only Friday, Saturday and Sunday have specific signs and the sign for Friday has developed from the fingerspelled F.

How to understand the photographs

Looking at the photographs

As we said earlier, it is impossible to learn to sign from a book. However, we do hope that you will find the photographs in this book a useful guide to refer to while you are taking a course in BSL.

Below is the photograph of the sign for 'autumn'. The English meaning is written below the photograph. The diagram in the top right-hand corner of the photograph shows exactly the handshape you should make. Where you use both hands to make the sign, and need a different handshape for each, we have shown both handshapes. Right-handed people should use the handshape in the top of each photograph for their right hand. If there is another handshape diagram below it, that is the handshape for the left hand. If you are left-handed, reverse them. The red line with an arrow shows the direction in which your hand should move, and how it should move. For example, for this sign your hands should both move downwards in a wavy pattern from left to right.

If there are two handshapes shown, but the sign is made with one hand, that means your handshape changes during the sign.

There is extra information underneath some photographs. The letters **DV,** for example, mean that the word is a directional verb (see page 13 for more information). Occasionally we have added a few words to clarify the meaning of a sign.

Autumn `Pic 1`

Autumn `Pic 2`

Pairs or groups of photographs that illustrate one sign

In many cases we have used more than one photograph to illustrate a sign. Where we have done this, there is a triangular arrow between the photographs, and they are labelled 'Pic 1', 'Pic 2', 'Pic 3', and so on. Examples of this are 'jacket' on page 32 and 'Italy' on page 38.

Photographs of alternative signs for the same English word

BSL has many regional variations and it is common for there to be more than one sign with the same meaning. We have not illustrated all of the signs for each English word, but where two different signs are frequently used, we have shown both of them. Where this has happened, we have labelled the photographs 'A' and 'B'. An example of this is 'before' on page 195.

The signs

Animal

Bird

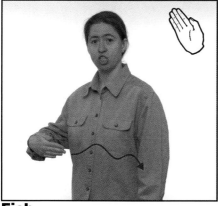

Fish

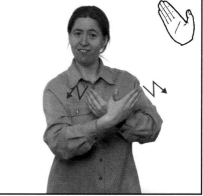

Butterfly

Spider

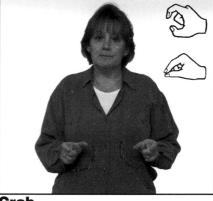

Crab

23

Dog

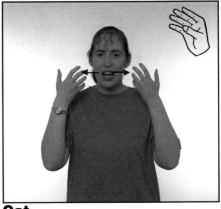

Cat

Mouse

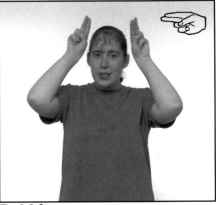

Rabbit

Horse

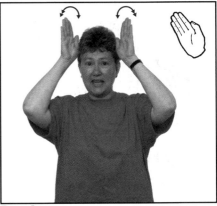

Donkey

Pig

Hen

Sheep

Cow

Deer

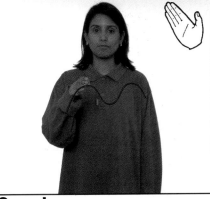

Camel

Lion — Pic 1

Lion — Pic 2

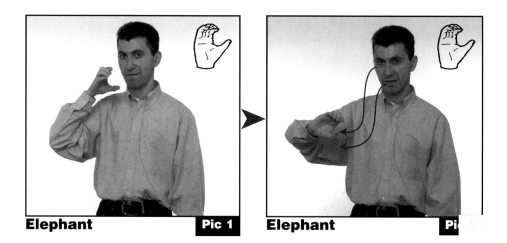

Elephant — Pic 1

Elephant — Pi

Snake — Pic 1

Snake — Pi

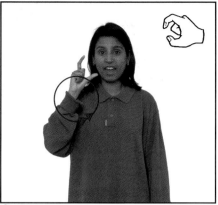

Colour

Orange

Red

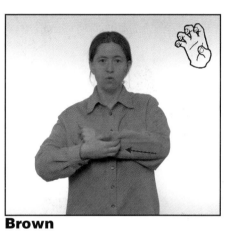

Brown

Yellow `Pic 1` **Yellow** `Pic 2`

Black

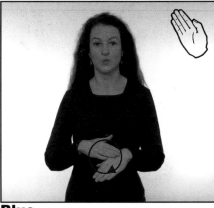

Blue

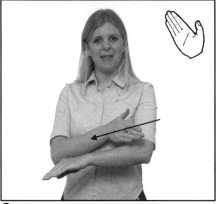

Green

Pink

White　　　　Pic 1

White　　　　Pic 2

Gold — Pic 1   **Gold** — Pic 2

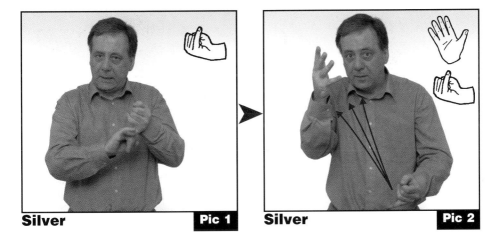

Silver — Pic 1   **Silver** — Pic 2

Clothes

Hat

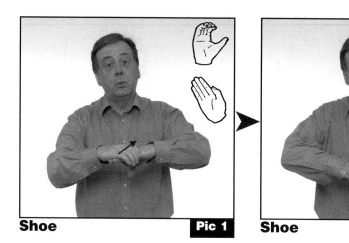

Shoe Pic 1

Shoe Pic 2

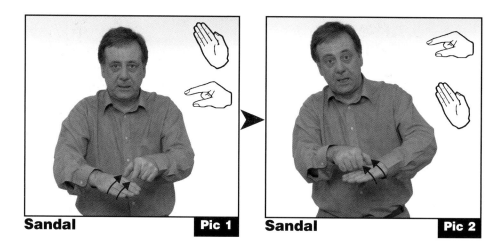

Sandal Pic 1

Sandal Pic 2

Boots

Socks

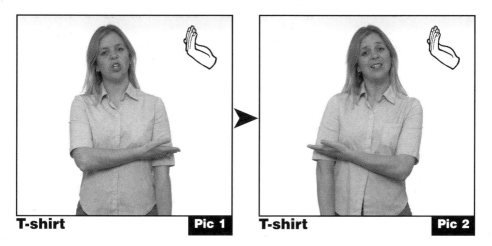

T-shirt Pic 1 **T-shirt** Pic 2

Jeans

Skirt

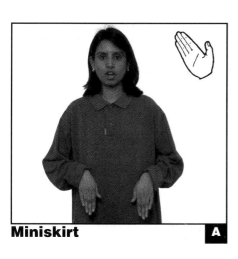

Miniskirt A

Miniskirt B

Dress

Shirt

Jacket `Pic 1`

Jacket `Pic 2`

Tie

Shorts

Jumper Pic 1

Jumper Pic 2

Deaf

Hard of hearing

Deafened Pic 1

Deafened Pic 2

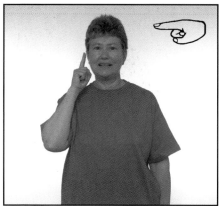

Hearing

Hearing aid

Sign language Pic 1

Sign language Pic 2

Lipread DV

Blind

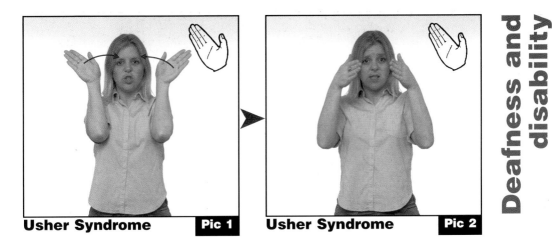

Usher Syndrome Pic 1

Usher Syndrome Pic 2

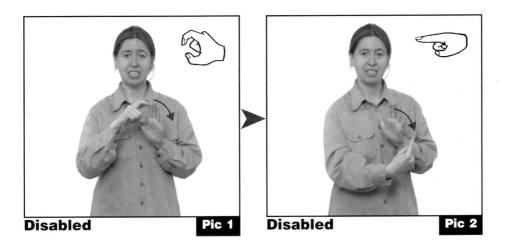

Disabled Pic 1

Disabled Pic 2

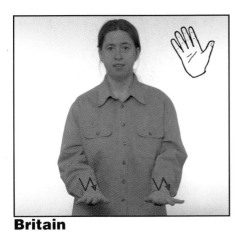

Britain

England

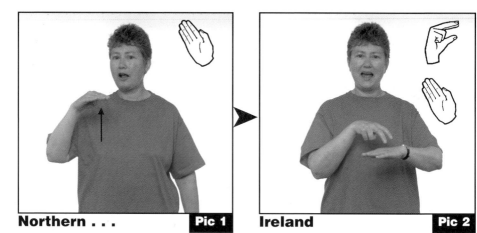

Northern . . . `Pic 1`　**Ireland** `Pic 2`

Pic 1 means *north* or *northern*. Pic 2 is the sign for *Ireland* when you talk about *Northern Ireland*. The sign for the *Republic of Ireland* is on page 37.

Scotland

Wales

Countries

Europe

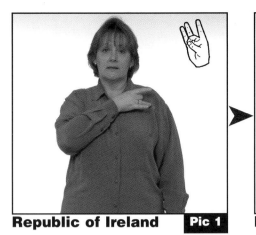

Republic of Ireland `Pic 1`

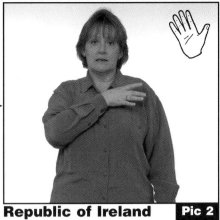

Republic of Ireland `Pic 2`

The sign for *Northern Ireland* is on page 36.

Sweden `Pic 1`

Sweden `Pic 2`

Norway

Denmark

37

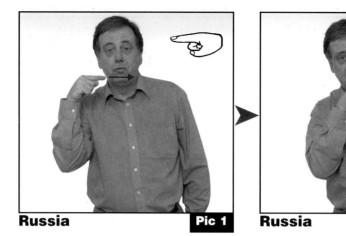

Russia Pic 1

Russia Pic 2

France

Germany

Italy Pic 1

Italy Pic 2

Greece

India

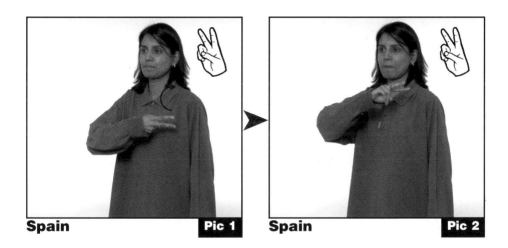

Spain `Pic 1`

Spain `Pic 2`

Portugal `Pic 1`

Portugal `Pic 2`

39

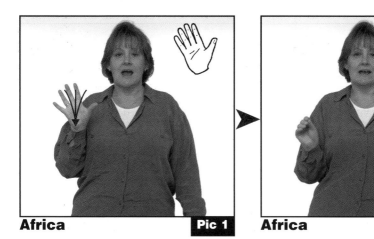

Africa Pic 1

Africa Pic 2

Australia Pic 1

Australia Pic 2

New . . . Pic 1

. . . Zealand Pic 2

China

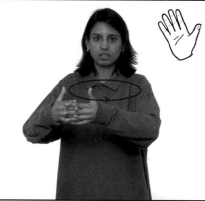

United States of America

Japan `Pic 1`

Japan `Pic 2`

Breakfast

Toast

Bacon

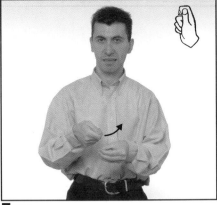

Egg

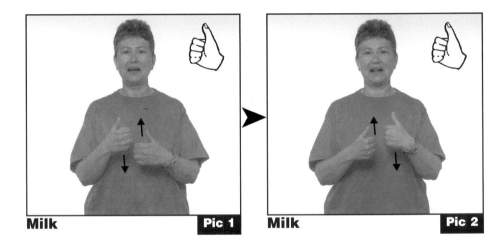

Milk Pic 1

Milk Pic 2

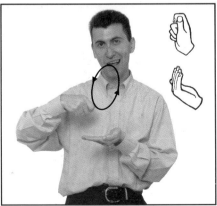

Cereal

Ice cream

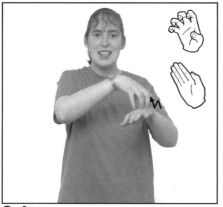

Cake

Biscuit

Bread

Sandwich

Chocolate

Café

Spoon

Knife

Fork

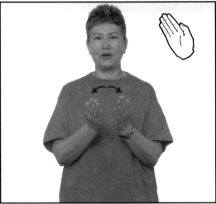

Menu

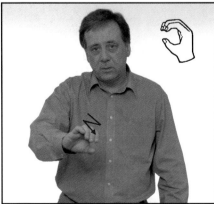

Salt/pepper

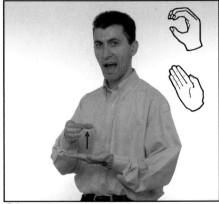

Glass

44

Plate

Bowl

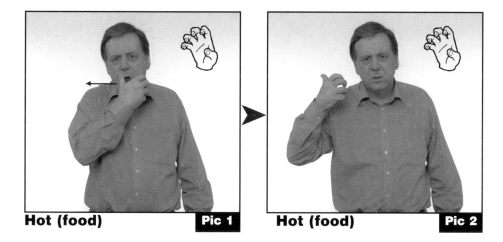

Hot (food) `Pic 1`

Hot (food) `Pic 2`

Sweet

Bitter

Food and drink

45

Dinner/restaurant

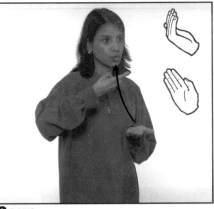

Soup

Fish (to eat)

Meat

Salad

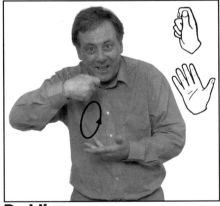

Pudding

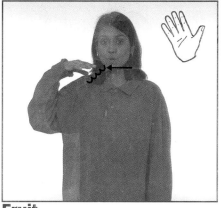

Fruit

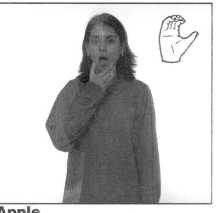

Apple

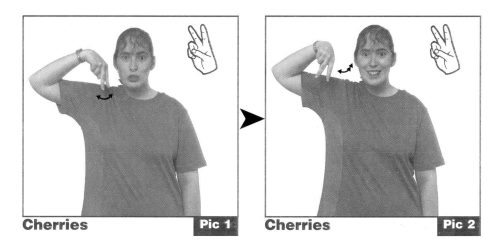

Cherries | Pic 1

Cherries | Pic 2

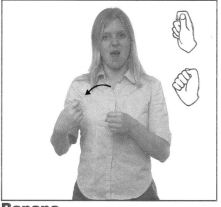

Banana

Melon

Peach

Vegetable

Tomato

Onion

Potato

Carrot

Pea Pic 1   **Pea** Pic 2

Pasta Pic 1   **Pasta** Pic 2

Rice

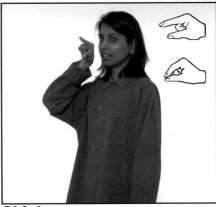

Chicken

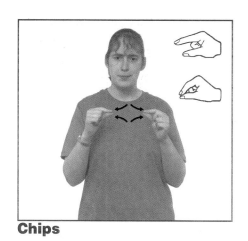

Chips

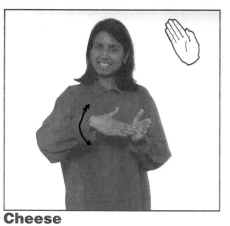

Cheese

Picnic Pic 1

Picnic Pic 2

Ice Pic 1

Ice Pic 2

50

Cream   Pic 1

Cream   Pic 2

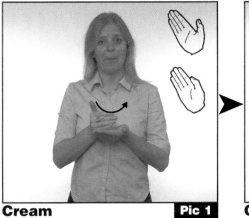

Sugar

Jam

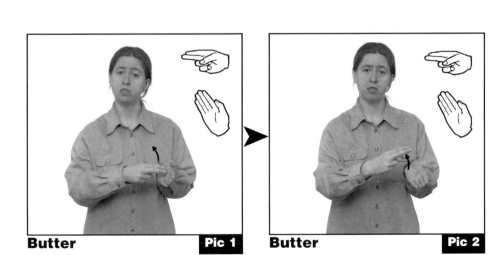

Butter   Pic 1

Butter   Pic 2

51

Nuts

Drink

Coffee

Tea

Wine

Beer

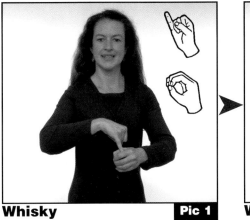

Whisky `Pic 1` **Whisky** `Pic 2`

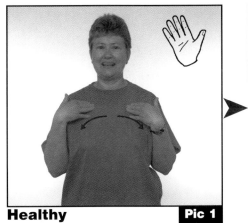

Healthy `Pic 1` **Healthy** `Pic 2`

Ill **Cough**

53

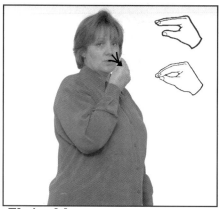

Flu/cold

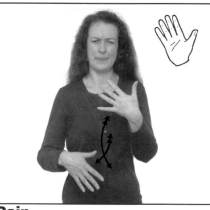

Pain

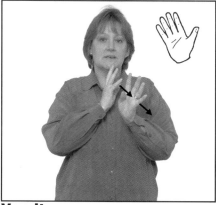

Vomit

Doctor

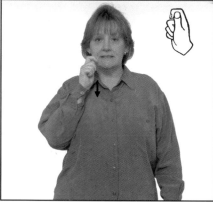

Dentist

Nurse

Emergency

Hospital

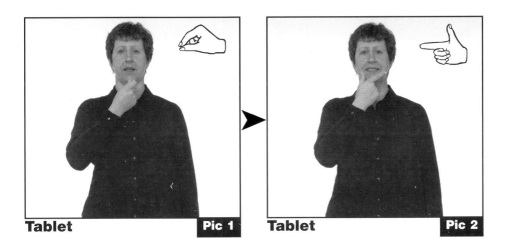

Tablet `Pic 1`

Tablet `Pic 2`

Medicine

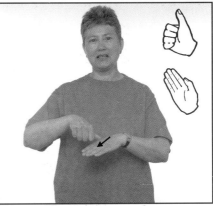

Operation

55

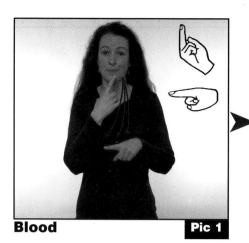

Blood — Pic 1

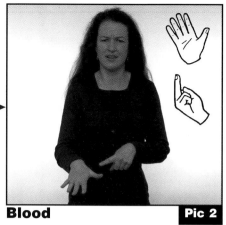

Blood — Pic 2

Heart

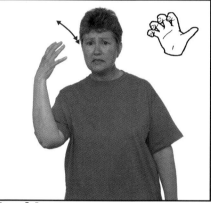

Accident

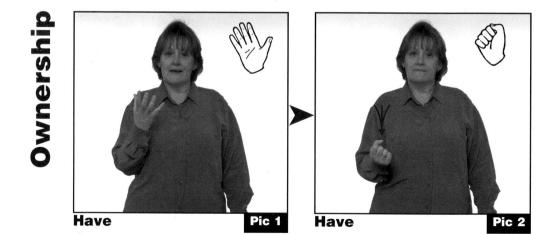

Have — Pic 1

Have — Pic 2

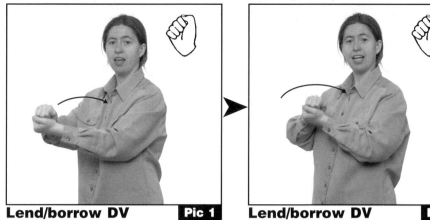

Lend/borrow DV `Pic 1` **Lend/borrow DV** `Pic 2`

This sign starts from the person lending and moves towards the person borrowing.

Keep

Buy

Sell `Pic 1` **Sell** `Pic 2`

Home

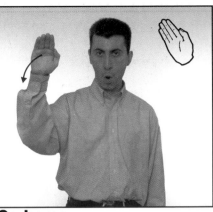

Go home

Address

House

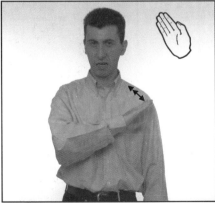

Garden/park

Flower

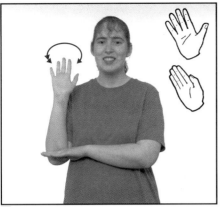

Tree

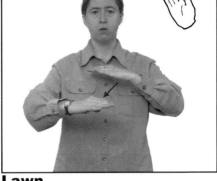

Lawn

Rubbish Pic 1

Rubbish Pic 2

Neighbour Pic 1

Neighbour Pic 2

Dirty Pic 1

Dirty Pic 2

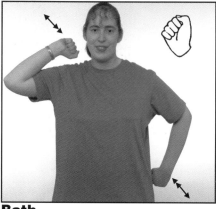

Bath

Soap

Water

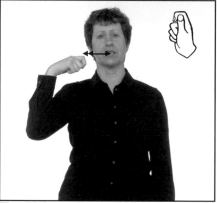

Toothbrush

Bed

Blanket

Duvet

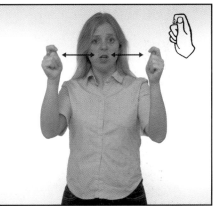

Curtains

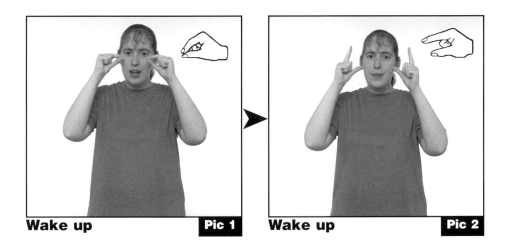

Wake up `Pic 1`

Wake up `Pic 2`

Go to sleep Pic 1

Go to sleep Pic 2

Asleep

Door

Chain Pic 1

Chain Pic 2

62

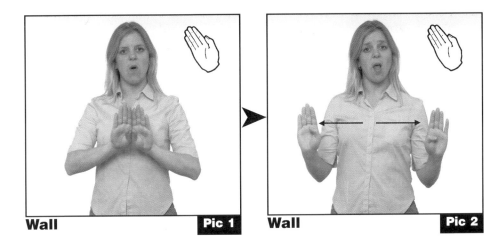

Wall Pic 1   **Wall** Pic 2

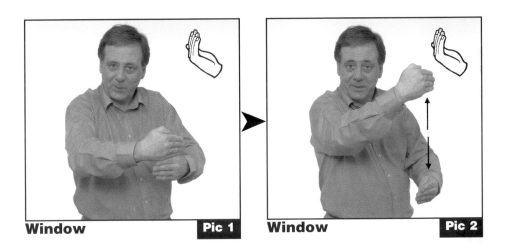

Window Pic 1   **Window** Pic 2

Corner

Kitchen

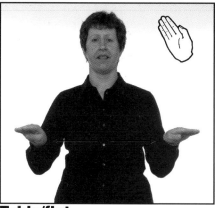

Table/flat

Either a flat surface, or a flat to live in.

Chair

Cupboard Pic 1

Cupboard Pic 2

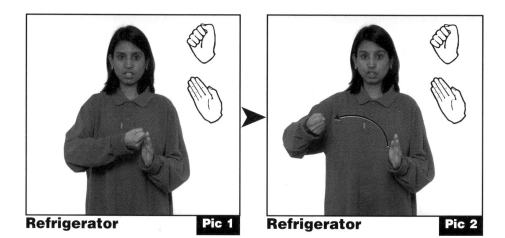

Refrigerator Pic 1

Refrigerator Pic 2

Cooker

Washing machine

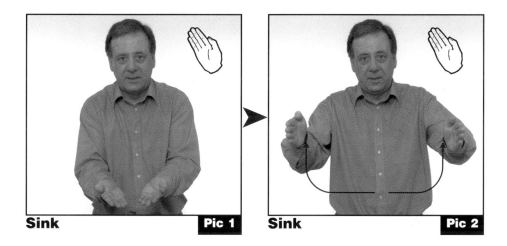

Sink | Pic 1

Sink | Pic 2

Toilet

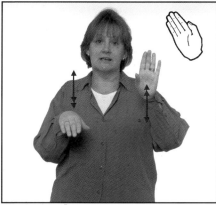

Decorating

65

Sweep

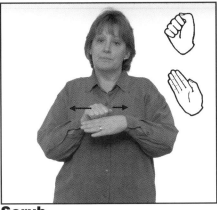

Scrub

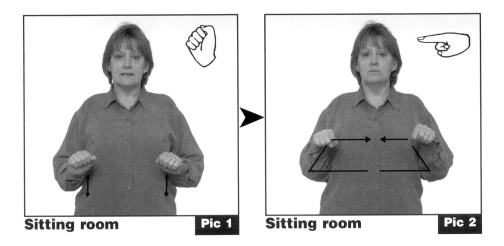

Sitting room Pic 1

Sitting room Pic 2

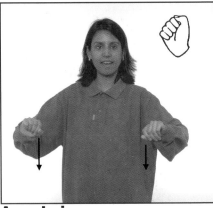

Armchair

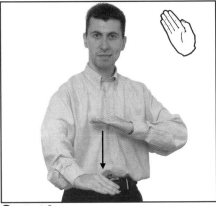

Carpet

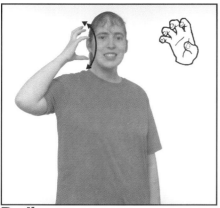

Radio

Sofa

Hall Pic 1

Hall Pic 2

Attic Pic 1

Attic Pic 2

67

Stairs

Electricity

Gas

Lights

Money

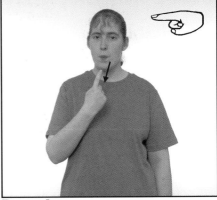

Pound

Penny Pic 1   **Penny** Pic 2

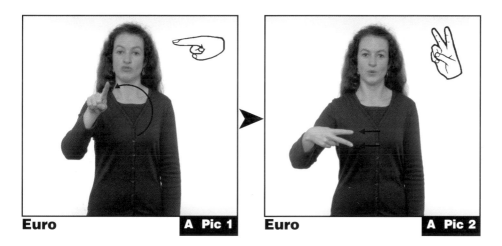

Euro A Pic 1   **Euro** A Pic 2

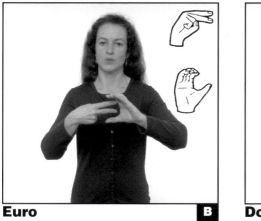

Euro B

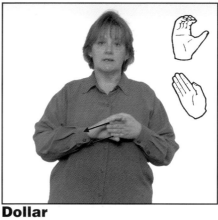

Dollar

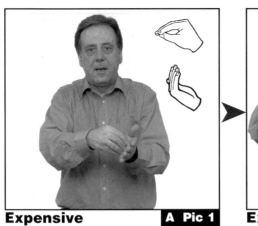

Expensive A Pic 1

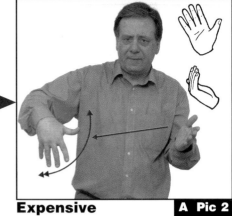

Expensive A Pic 2

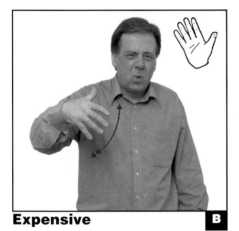

Expensive B

Cheap

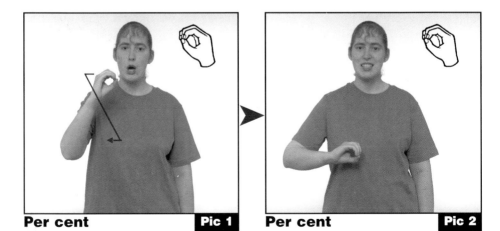

Per cent Pic 1

Per cent Pic 2

Bank

Insurance

Spend | Pic 1

Spend | Pic 2

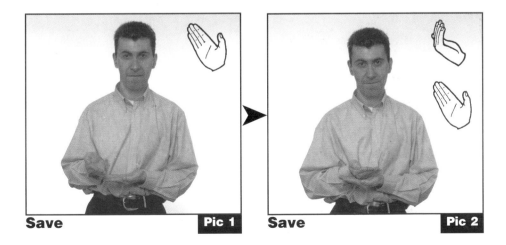

Save | Pic 1

Save | Pic 2

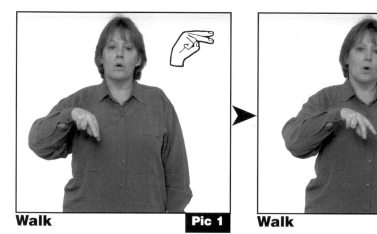

Walk — Pic 1

Walk — Pic 2

Run — Pic 1

Run — Pic 2

Jump — A

Jump — B

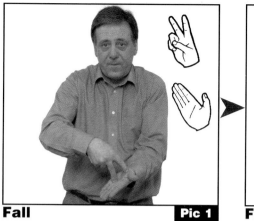

Fall | Pic 1

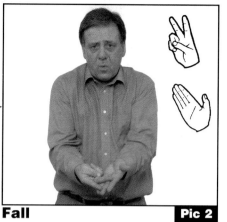

Fall | Pic 2

Dive

Stand

Sit

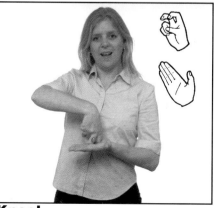

Kneel

Lead/guide — Pic 1

Lead/guide — Pic 2

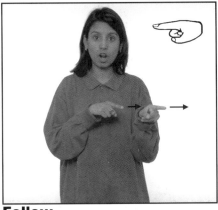

Follow

Lie down

Place/area

London/noise

74

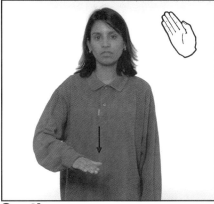

South

The sign for *north* is on page 36.

East

West

On (as in *on top of*)

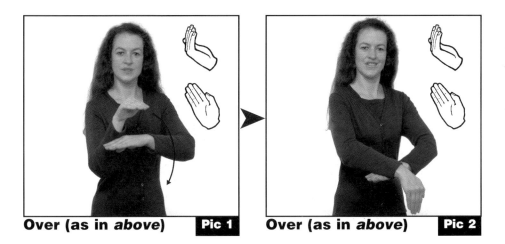

Over (as in *above*)   Pic 1

Over (as in *above*)   Pic 2

75

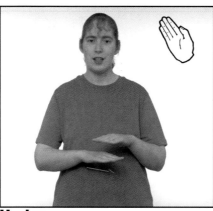

Under

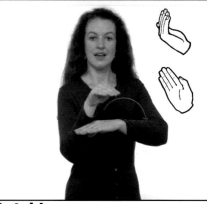

Outside

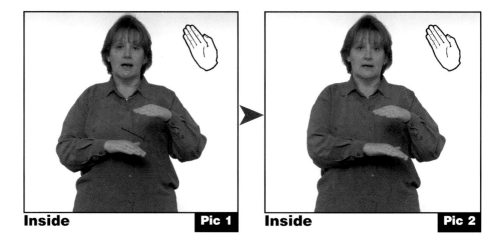

Inside Pic 1

Inside Pic 2

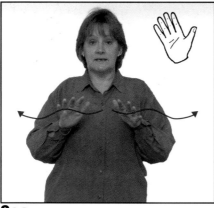

Sea

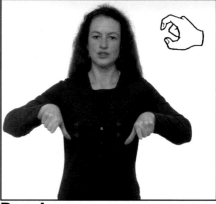

Beach

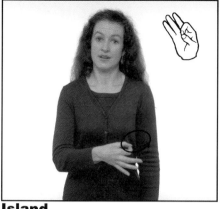

Island

Forest

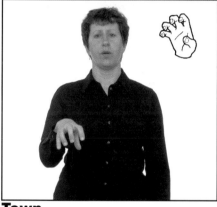

Town

Village

Valley

Hill

Places

Road

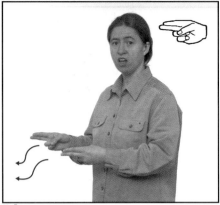

River

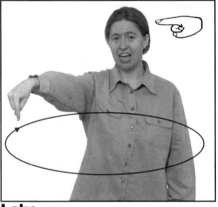

Lake

Mountain

Questions

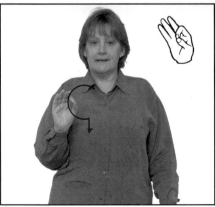

Question

Ask DV (see also page 13)

Answer Pic 1

Answer Pic 2

Who

What

How

When

Where

Why/because

Reason

Which

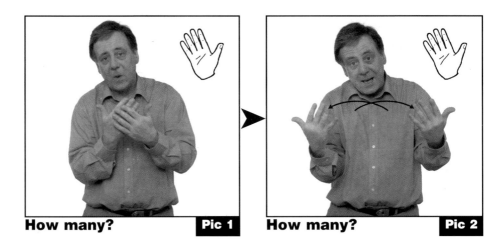

How many?   Pic 1

How many?   Pic 2

80

Polite — Pic 1

Polite — Pic 2

Rude

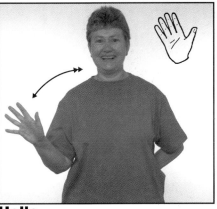

Hello

Please — Pic 1

Please — Pic 2

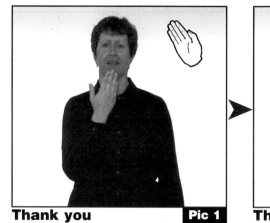

Thank you `Pic 1`

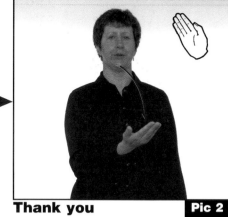

Thank you `Pic 2`

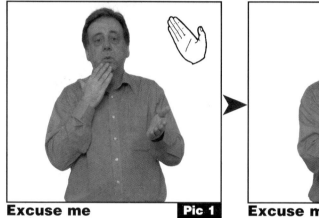

Excuse me `Pic 1`

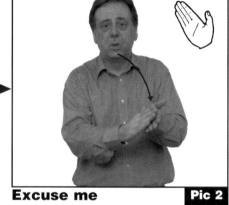

Excuse me `Pic 2`

How are you? `Pic 1`

How are you? `Pic 2`

82

Sorry

Goodbye

Sport Pic 1

Sport Pic 2

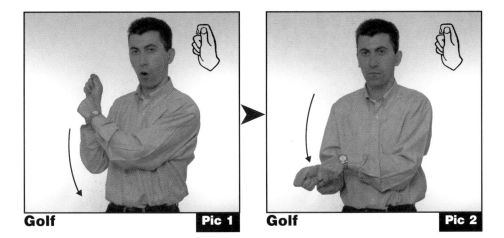

Golf Pic 1

Golf Pic 2

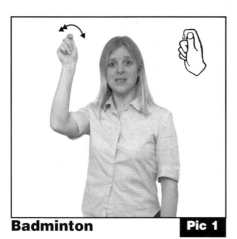

Badminton | Pic 1

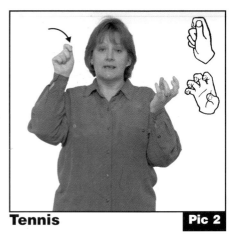

Tennis | Pic 2

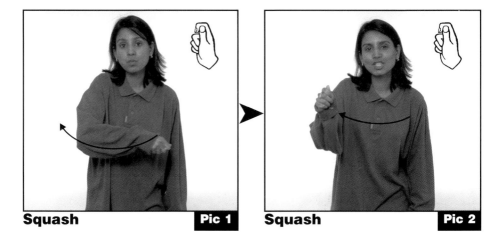

Squash | Pic 1

Squash | Pic 2

Cricket | Pic 1

Cricket | Pic 2

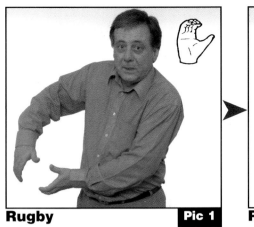

Rugby `Pic 1`

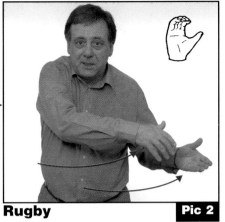

Rugby `Pic 2`

Ball

Football

Goal

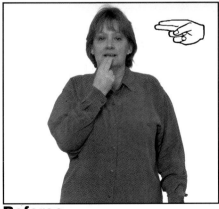

Referee

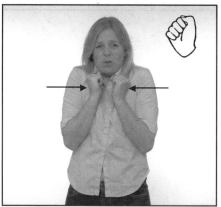

Crowd

Horse riding

Cycling

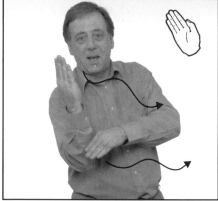

Sailing

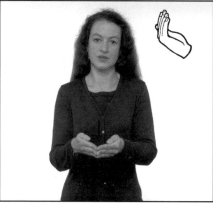

Boat

Skiing

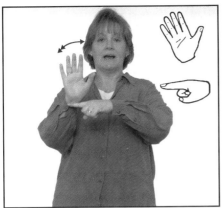

Cinema

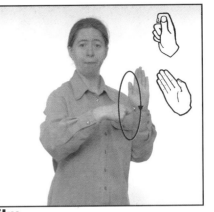

Film

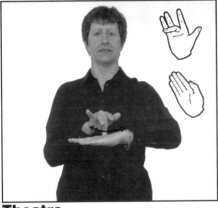

Theatre

Play (at the theatre)

Actor

Bar/pub

Dance   Pic 1

Dance   Pic 2

Bottle   Pic 1

Bottle   Pic 2

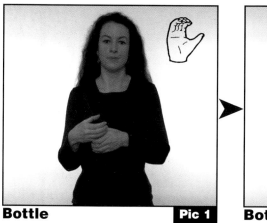

Sing   Pic 1

Sing   Pic 2

Party

Drunk

Knit

Sew

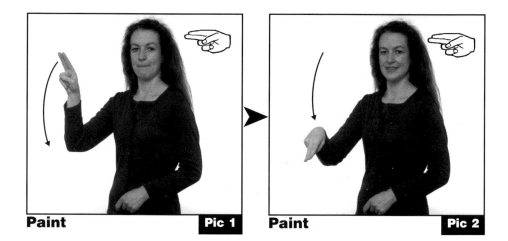

Paint   Pic 1   **Paint**   Pic 2

89

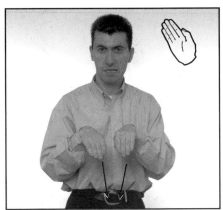
Sewing machine

Camera/photograph

Photograph (snapshot)

Dream/imagine

See DV   A   Pic 1

See DV   A   Pic 2

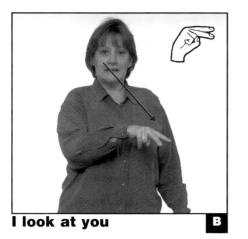

I look at you B

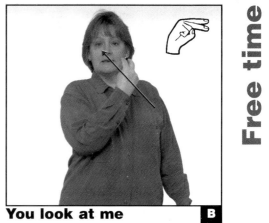

You look at me B

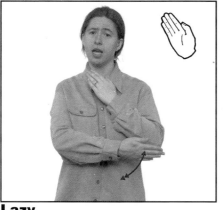

Lazy

Rest

Relax Pic 1

Relax Pic 2

91

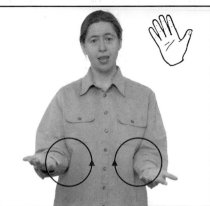

Play (a game)

Competition

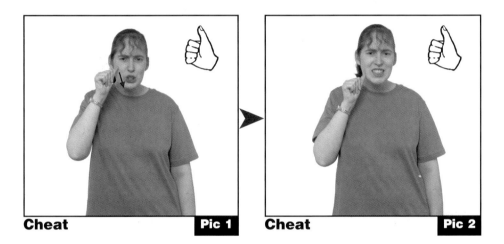

Cheat   `Pic 1`

Cheat   `Pic 2`

Win   `Pic 1`

Win   `Pic 2`

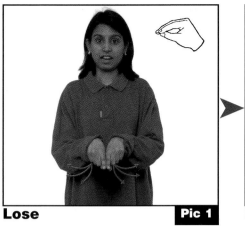

Lose   `Pic 1`

Lose   `Pic 2`

Programme

Video recorder

Video tape   `A`

Video tape   `B`

93

Free time

Record
(from television)   `A  Pic 1`

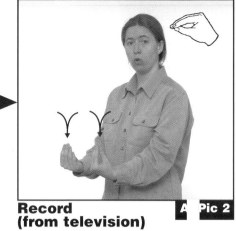

Record
(from television)   `A  Pic 2`

Record (music)   `B  Pic 1`

Record (music)   `B  Pic 2`

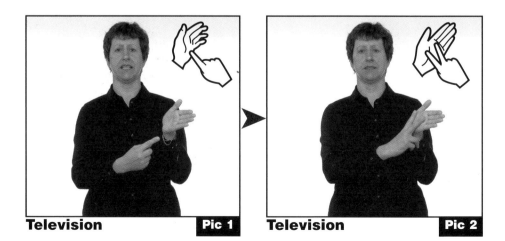

Television   `Pic 1`

Television   `Pic 2`

94

Queue `Pic 1`

Queue `Pic 2`

Book (reserve)

Shop

Ticket

Birthday

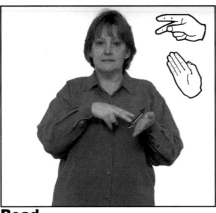

Read

Book (to read)

Library   `Pic 1`

Library   `Pic 2`

Newspaper   `Pic 1`

Newspaper   `Pic 2`

Tell a story DV   `Pic 1`

Tell a story DV   `Pic 2`

Music   `Pic 1`

Music   `Pic 2`

Help DV   `Pic 1`

Help DV   `Pic 2`

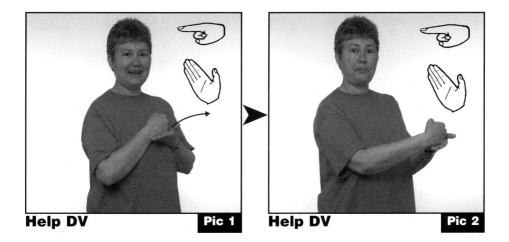

Association | Pic 1

Association | Pic 2

Community

Volunteer

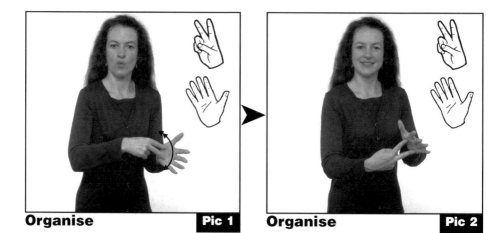

Organise | Pic 1

Organise | Pic 2

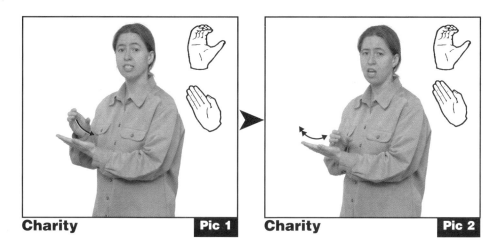

Charity **Pic 1**

Charity **Pic 2**

Few

Plenty

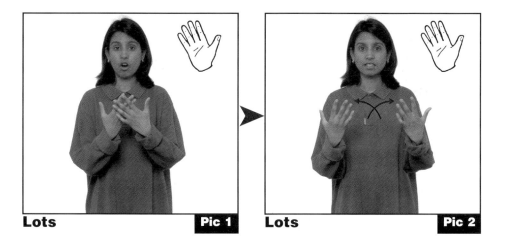

Lots **Pic 1**

Lots **Pic 2**

Nothing

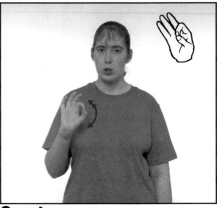

Quarter

Half

Number

First

Second

Third

Weigh

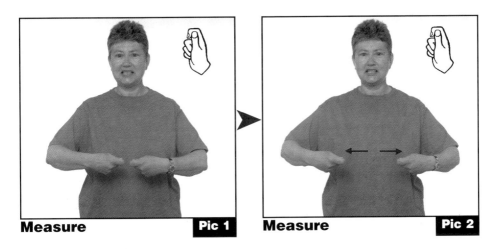

Measure Pic 1

Measure Pic 2

I

You (he/she/it)

This sign means you, he, she or it, depending on whom you point to.

My

Mine

The sign for *your* or *yours*, is made in the same way but the knuckles and palm of your hand face the person you are talking to.

Myself   Pic 1

Myself   Pic 2

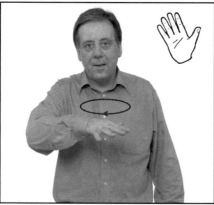

Family

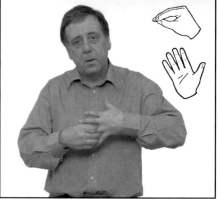

Husband/wife

People

Father

Mother — Pic 1

Mother — Pic 2

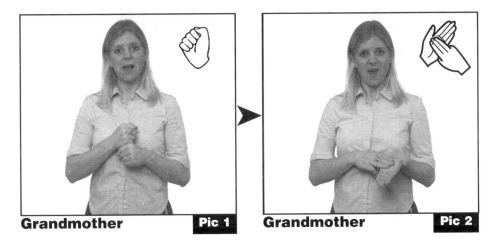

Grandmother — Pic 1

Grandmother — Pic 2

103

Grandfather — Pic 1   **Grandfather** — Pic 2

Brother

Sister

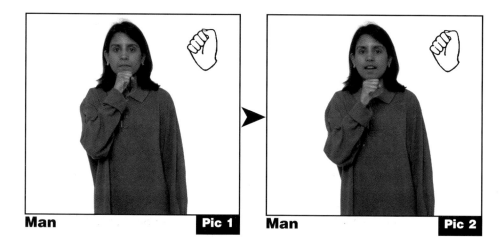

Man — Pic 1   **Man** — Pic 2

Woman

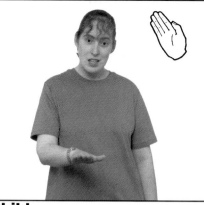

Child

Uncle

Aunt

Nephew

Niece

105

Son

Daughter

Cousin | Pic 1

Cousin | Pic 2

Person

Meet | A

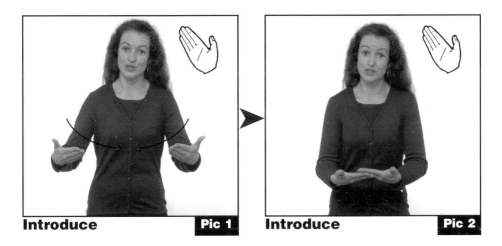

Meet B Pic 1

Meet B Pic 2

Introduce Pic 1

Introduce Pic 2

Single Pic 1

Single Pic 2

Friend

Gay

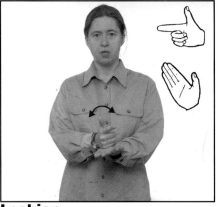

Lesbian

Born

Die

Boy

Girl

Baby

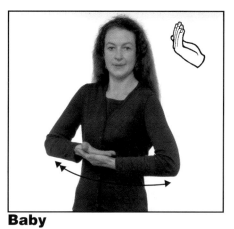

Grow up

Name

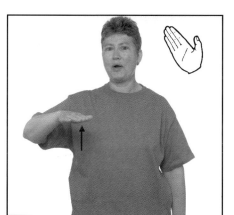

Marry Pic 1

Marry Pic 2

Divorce　**Pic 1**　**Divorce**　**Pic 2**

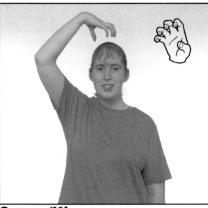

Queen/King　**Government**

Prime Minister　**Pic 1**　**Prime Minister**　**Pic 2**

Party (political)

Council

Educate `Pic 1`

Educate `Pic 2`

Teach DV

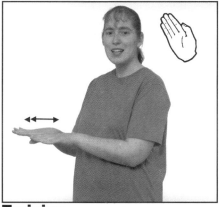

Training

Know

Clear

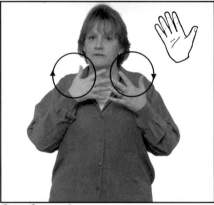

Confused

Slow down!

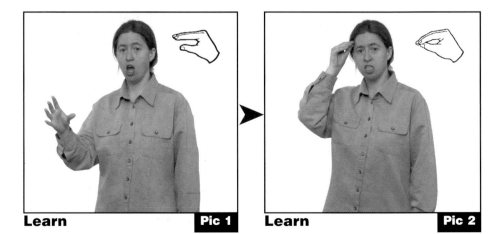

Learn   Pic 1

Learn   Pic 2

Forget — Pic 1   Forget — Pic 2

Lesson — A

Lesson — B

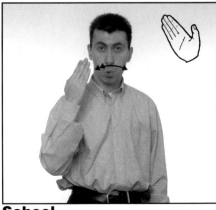

School

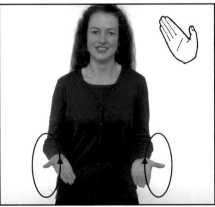

Encourage

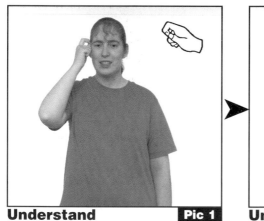

Understand `Pic 1`

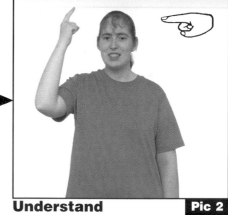

Understand `Pic 2`

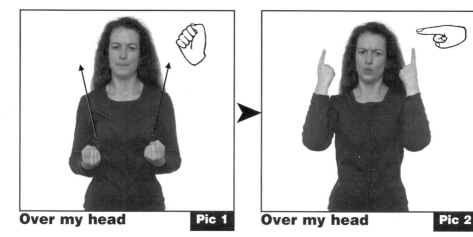

Over my head `Pic 1`

Over my head `Pic 2`

Attention

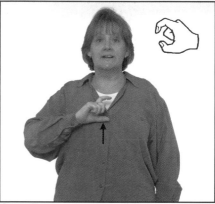

Confident

College

Degree/diploma

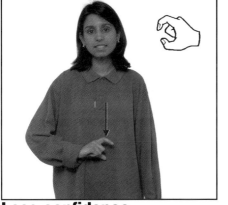

Lose confidence

Gallaudet . . . `Pic 1`

Gallaudet . . . `Pic 2`

. . . University `Pic 3`

115

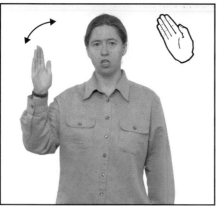

Lecture

Stupid (person)

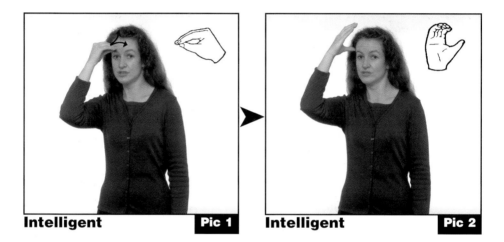

Intelligent Pic 1

Intelligent Pic 2

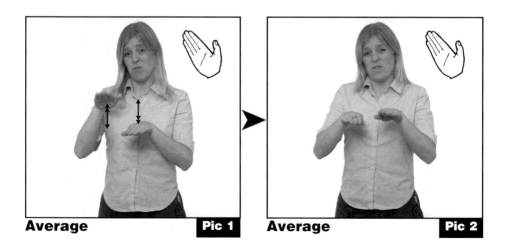

Average Pic 1

Average Pic 2

Exams Pic 1

Exams Pic 2

Fail Pic 1

Fail Pic 2

Pass

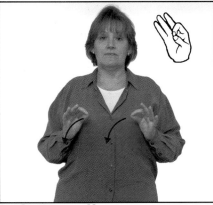

Defer/put off

Traffic

Car

Coach

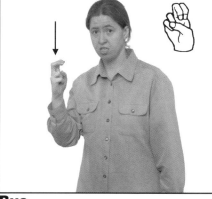

Bus

Engine

Drive

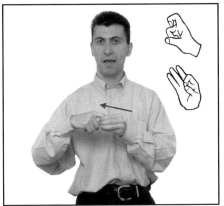

Caravan

Petrol

Crash Pic 1

Crash Pic 2

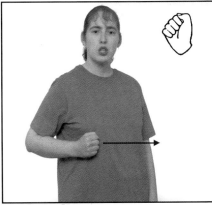

Train/railway

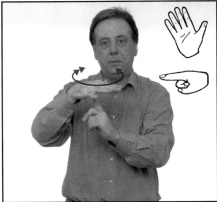

Helicopter

Aeroplane

Foreign/abroad

Far away

Language

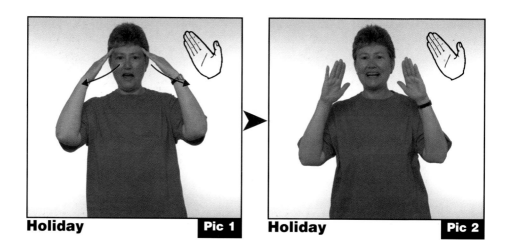

Holiday | Pic 1

Holiday | Pic 2

120

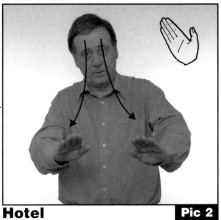

Hotel Pic 1

Hotel Pic 2

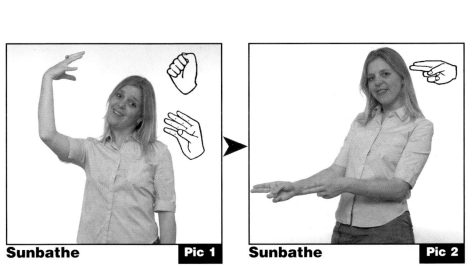

Sunbathe Pic 1

Sunbathe Pic 2

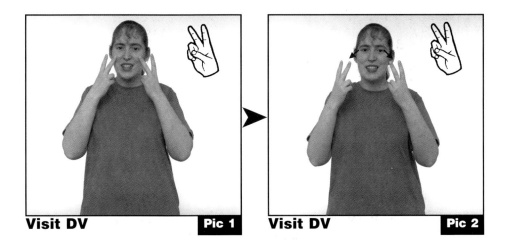

Visit DV Pic 1

Visit DV Pic 2

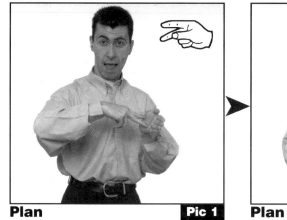
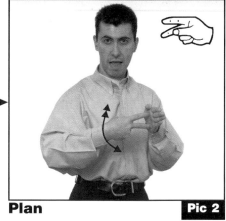

Plan | Pic 1

Plan | Pic 2

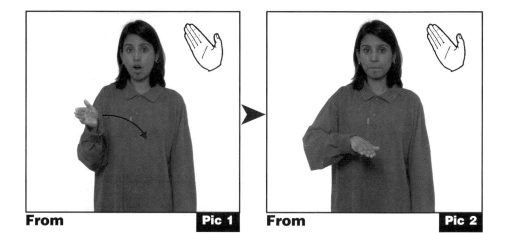

From | Pic 1

From | Pic 2

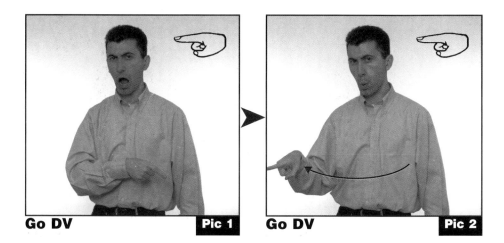

Go DV | Pic 1

Go DV | Pic 2

Between

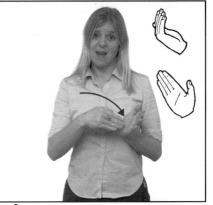

Arrive

Come   Pic 1   **Come**   Pic 2

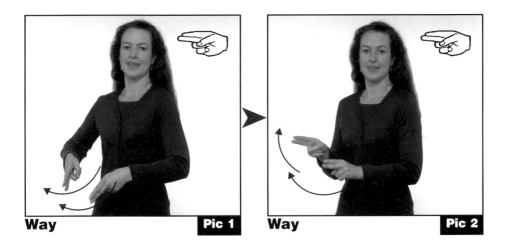

Way   Pic 1   **Way**   Pic 2

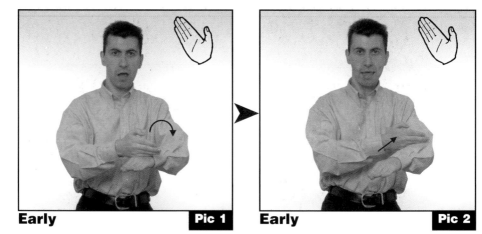

Early   Pic 1   **Early**   Pic 2

Late   Pic 1   **Late**   Pic 2

Weather

Sun

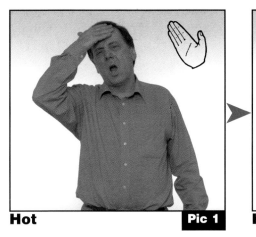

Hot Pic 1

Hot Pic 2

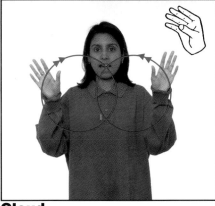

Cloud

Thunder/lightning

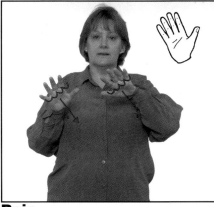

Rain

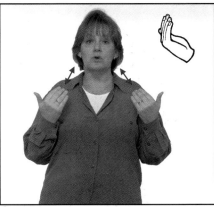

Cool

Cold

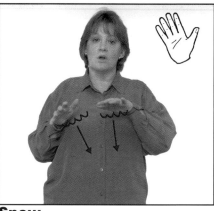

Snow

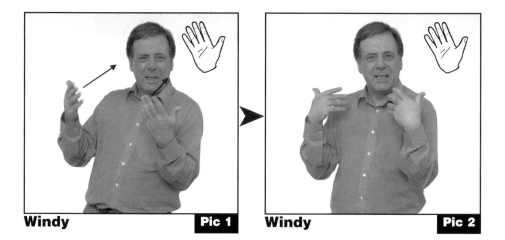

Windy | Pic 1

Windy | Pic 2

Fog

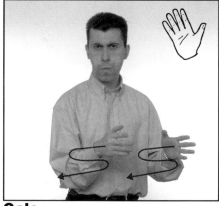

Gale

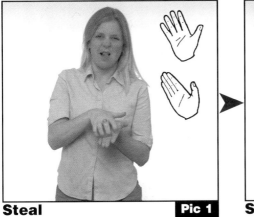

Steal · Pic 1

Steal · Pic 2

Burglar

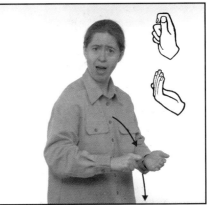

Fine (money)

Murder

Prison

127

Escape — Pic 1   **Escape** — Pic 2

Law — Pic 1   **Law** — Pic 2

Suspicious DV

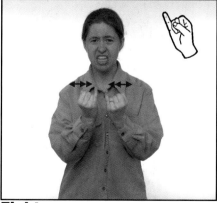

Fight

Proof

Guilty

Solicitor A Pic 1

Solicitor A Pic 2

Solicitor B

Judge

129

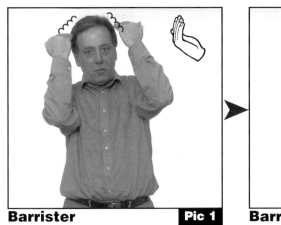

Barrister Pic 1

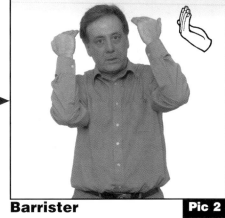

Barrister Pic 2

Police Pic 1

Police Pic 2

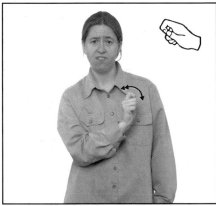

Detective

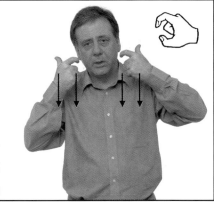

Court

Space

World

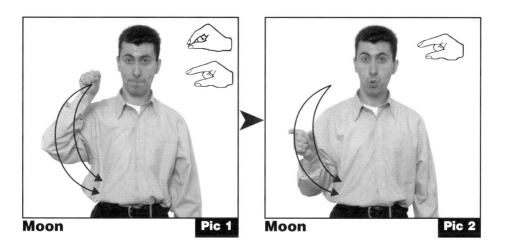

Moon Pic 1

Moon Pic 2

Star

Spaceship

Sunday

Monday

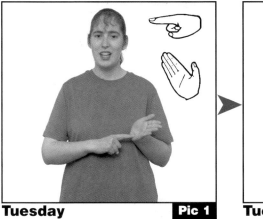
Tuesday | Pic 1

Tuesday | Pic 2

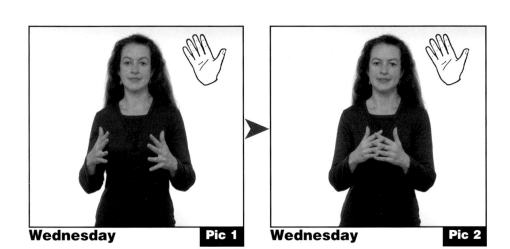
Wednesday | Pic 1

Wednesday | Pic 2

132

Thursday `Pic 1`

Thursday `Pic 2`

Friday

Saturday

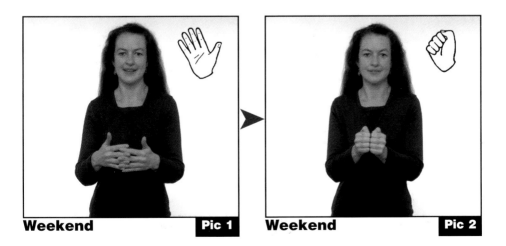

Weekend `Pic 1`

Weekend `Pic 2`

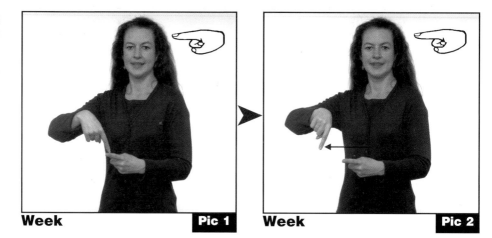

Week — Pic 1   Week — Pic 2

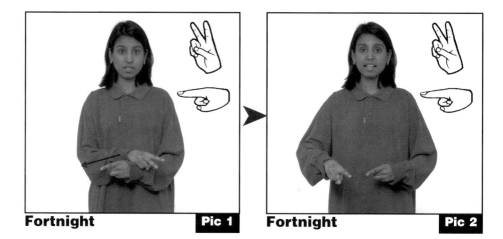

Fortnight — Pic 1   Fortnight — Pic 2

Day — Pic 1   Day — Pic 2

Month

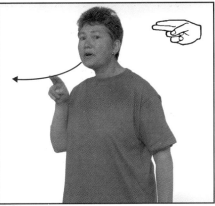

Afternoon

Morning Pic 1

Morning Pic 2

Evening

Night

Yesterday `Pic 1`

Yesterday `Pic 2`

Today

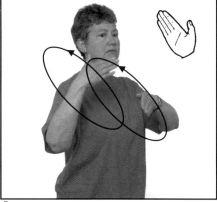

Ages ago

Tomorrow `Pic 1`

Tomorrow `Pic 2`

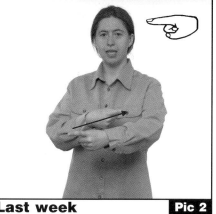

Last week Pic 1

Last week Pic 2

Next week

Future

Past Pic 1

Past Pic 2

Spring — Pic 1 · **Spring** — Pic 2

Autumn — Pic 1 · **Autumn** — Pic 2

Summer

Winter

Christmas `Pic 1`

Christmas `Pic 2`

Easter

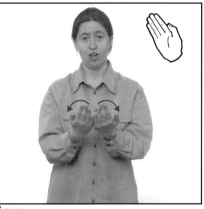

Diary

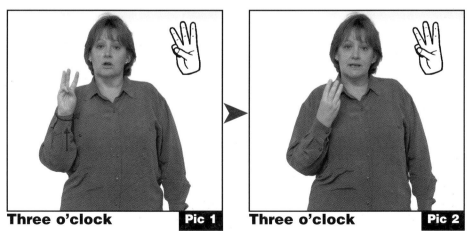

Three o'clock `Pic 1`

Three o'clock `Pic 2`

By holding up the right number of fingers and making the same hand movement, you can sign other times.

139

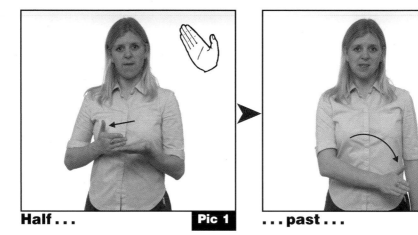

Half . . .   Pic 1

. . . past . . .   Pic 2

. . . three   Pic 3

Time

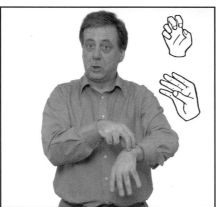

Wristwatch

Clock

140

Remember — Pic 1

Remember — Pic 2

Remind — Pic 1

Remind — Pic 2

Work

Office

Telephone DV

Telephone DV

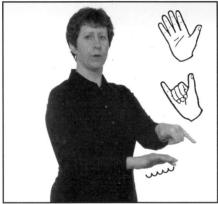

Textphone

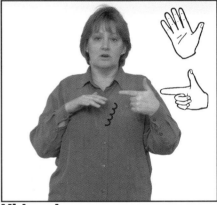

Videophone

Typetalk | **Pic 1**

Typetalk | **Pic 2**

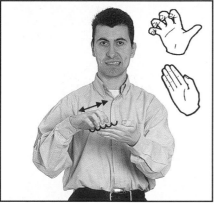

Portable textphone

Write

Envelope

Internet `Pic 1`

Internet `Pic 2`

Internet `Pic 3`

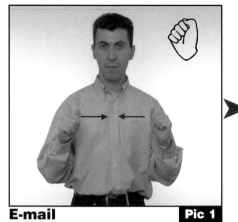 

E-mail Pic 1 **E-mail** Pic 2

 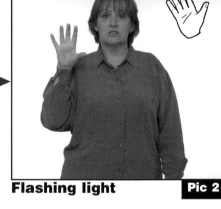

Flashing light Pic 1 **Flashing light** Pic 2

 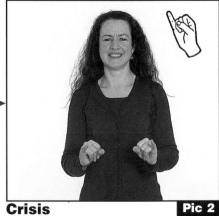

Crisis Pic 1 **Crisis** Pic 2

Computer Pic 1

Computer Pic 2

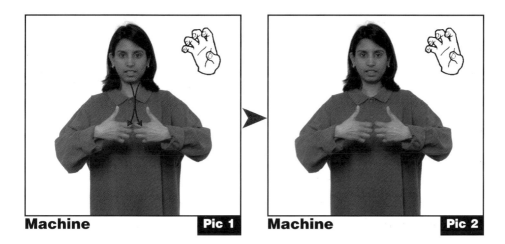

Machine Pic 1

Machine Pic 2

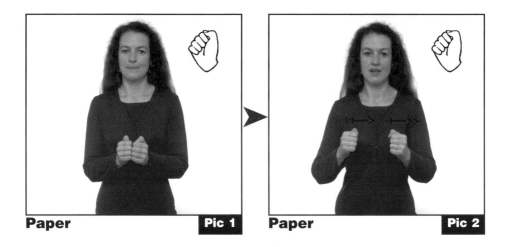

Paper Pic 1

Paper Pic 2

Letter Pic 1 | **Letter** Pic 2

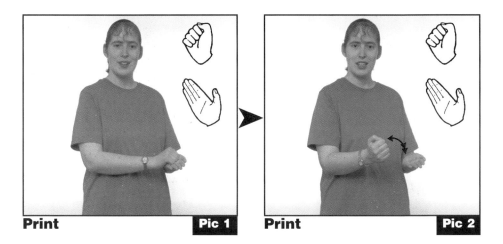

Print Pic 1 | **Print** Pic 2

 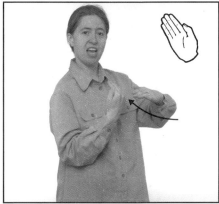

Fax (to someone) DV | **Fax (from someone) DV**

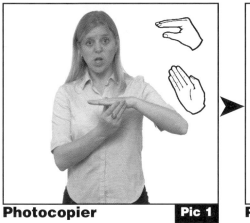

Photocopier `Pic 1`

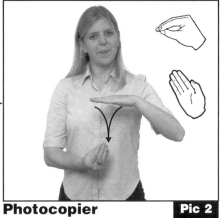

Photocopier `Pic 2`

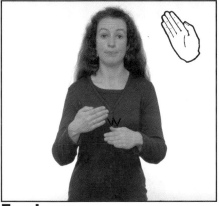

Employer

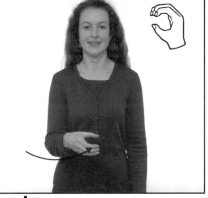

Employee

Advertise

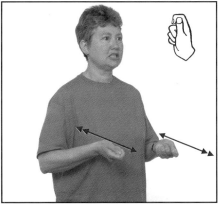

Administration

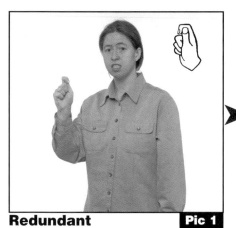

Redundant Pic 1

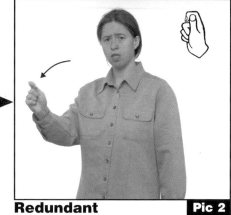

Redundant Pic 2

Dismiss Pic 1

Dismiss Pic 2

Unemployed Pic 1

Unemployed Pic 2

Meeting Pic 1

Meeting Pic 2

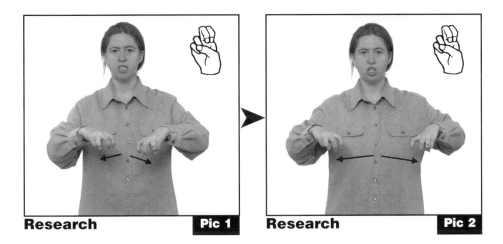

Research Pic 1

Research Pic 2

Agenda

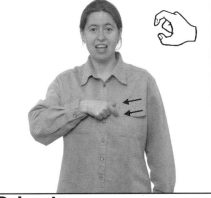

Delegate

Committee

Firefighter

Fire — Pic 1

Fire — Pic 2

Engineer

Farmer

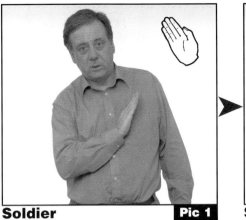

Soldier Pic 1

Soldier Pic 2

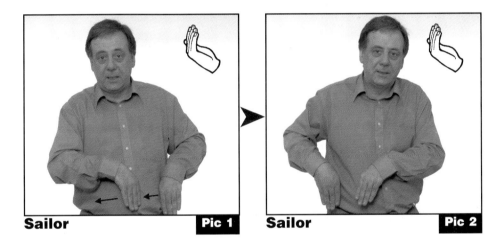

Sailor Pic 1

Sailor Pic 2

Service Pic 1

Service Pic 2

151

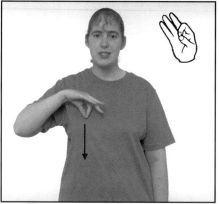

Profit

Salary

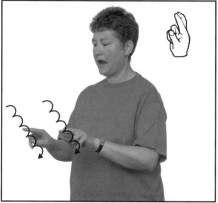

Accounts

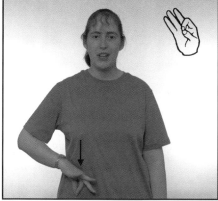

Benefit

Strike　　Pic 1

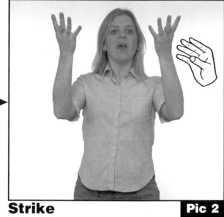

Strike　　Pic 2

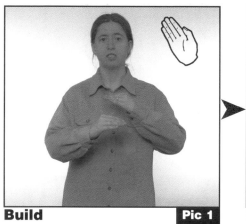

Build   **Pic 1**

Build   **Pic 2**

Factory

Make

Metal

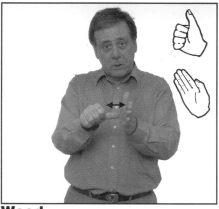

Wood

Repair

Busy

Routine — Pic 1   **Routine** — Pic 2

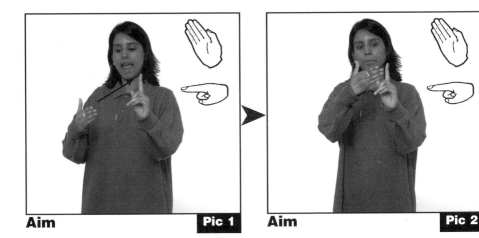

Aim — Pic 1   **Aim** — Pic 2

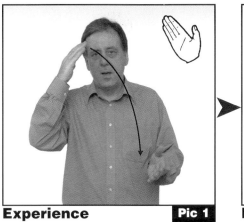

Experience `Pic 1`

Experience `Pic 2`

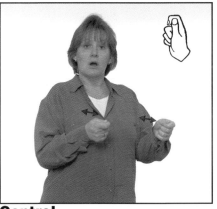

Control

Depend

Responsible

Improve

155

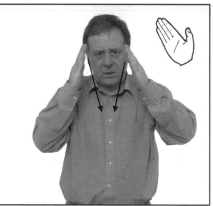

Concentrate

Analyse

Hard/difficult

Easy

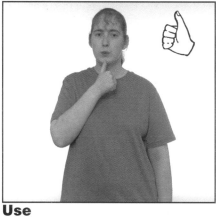

Use

Arrange

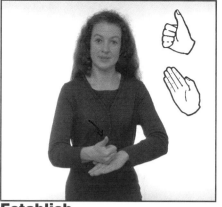

Establish

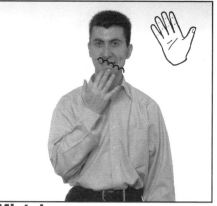

Mistake

Danger

Safety

Communicate

Typing

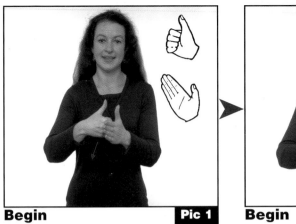

Begin — Pic 1

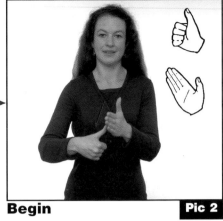

Begin — Pic 2

Finish

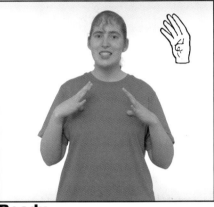

Ready

Deadline — Pic 1

Deadline — Pic 2

SpeedText `Pic 1`

SpeedText `Pic 2`

Videophone

Interpreter

Lipspeaker `Pic 1`

Lipspeaker `Pic 2`

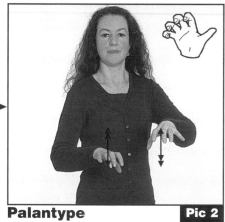

Palantype `Pic 1`

Palantype `Pic 2`

Character/personality

Feel

Same

All right

160

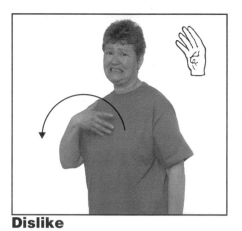
Dislike

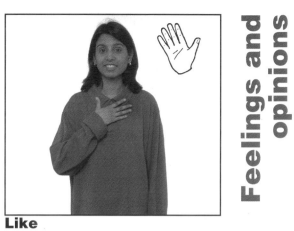
Like

Hate `Pic 1`

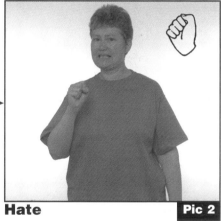
Hate `Pic 2`

Love

Sad

Depressed

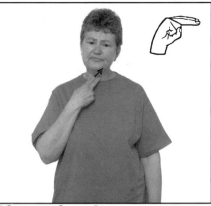

Disappointed

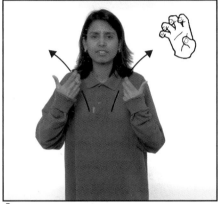

Angry

Forgive

Happy   Pic 1

Happy   Pic 2

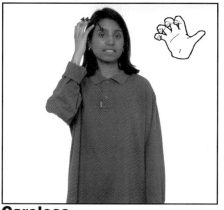

Careless

Careful

Frustrated Pic 1

Frustrated Pic 2

Cheeky

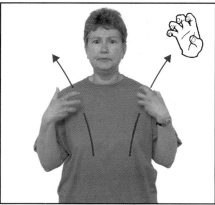

Aggressive

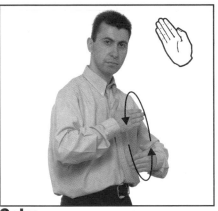

Calm

Afraid

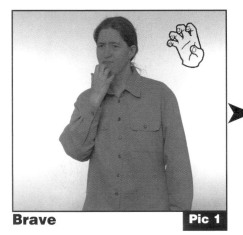

Brave Pic 1

Brave Pic 2

Sly

Honest

Worry

Funny/laugh

Shy **A**

Shy **B**

Embarrassed

Bored

Interesting/interested

Keen

Should/ought to

Shouldn't

Satisfied

Hope

Smile

Envy

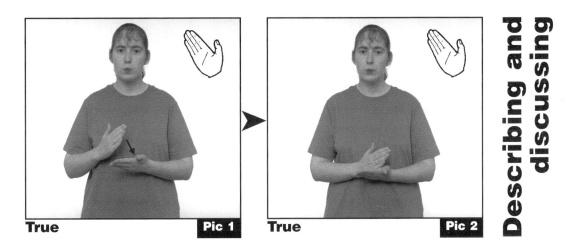

True — Pic 1

True — Pic 2

False — Pic 1

False — Pic 2

167

Sure

Correct

Lie (untruth) Pic 1

Lie (untruth) Pic 2

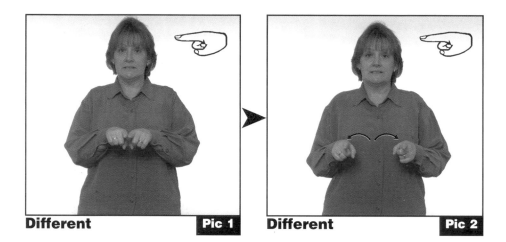

Different Pic 1

Different Pic 2

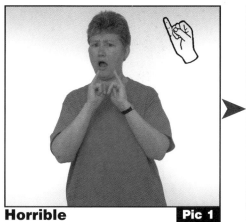

Horrible `Pic 1`

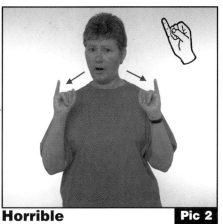

Horrible `Pic 2`

Nice

Brilliant

Good

Bad

Worse | Pic 1

Worse | Pic 2

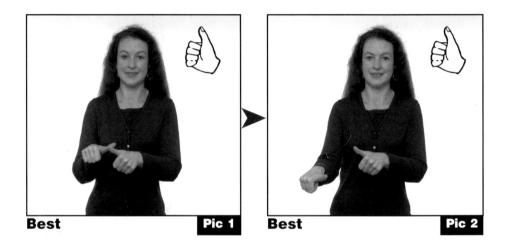

Best | Pic 1

Best | Pic 2

Better

Each

Alike | Pic 1

Alike | Pic 2

Some | Pic 1

Some | Pic 2

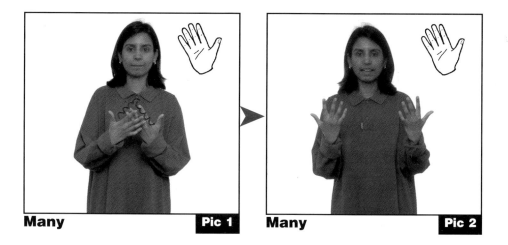

Many | Pic 1

Many | Pic 2

Describing and discussing

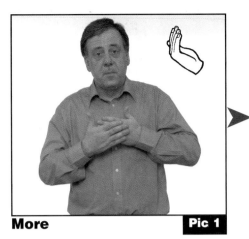

More — Pic 1

More — Pic 2

Every

Another/other

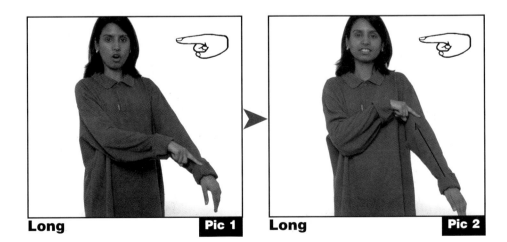

Long — Pic 1

Long — Pic 2

Short (in length) **A**

Short (in height) **B**

Tall

Small

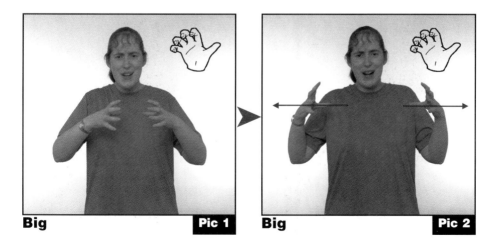

Big **Pic 1**

Big **Pic 2**

Tiny

No (naughty)   **A**

No (don't)   **B**

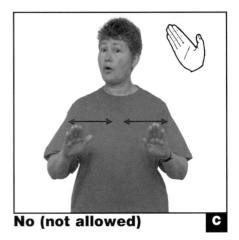

No (not allowed)   **C**

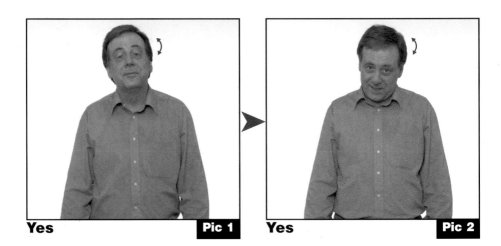

Yes   **Pic 1**

Yes   **Pic 2**

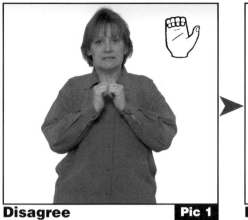

Disagree — Pic 1

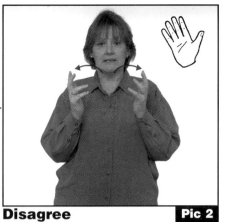

Disagree — Pic 2

Agree

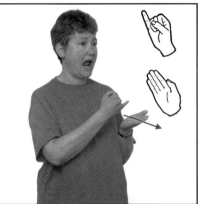

Against/object to

Refuse — A Pic 1

Refuse — A Pic 2

175

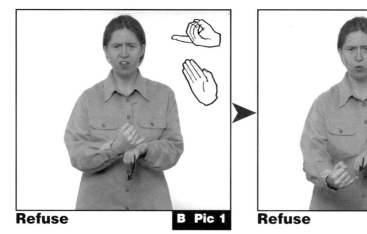

Refuse   B Pic 1

Refuse   B Pic 2

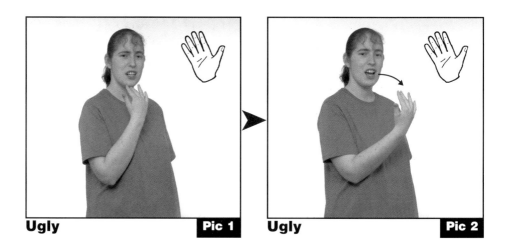

Ugly   Pic 1

Ugly   Pic 2

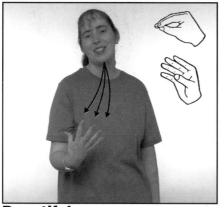

Beautiful

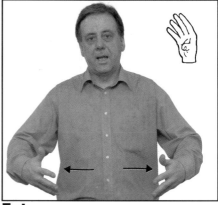

Fat

176

Thin

Perfect

Special

Strange

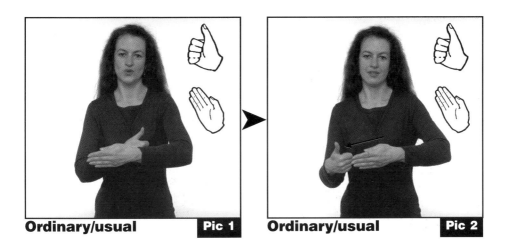

Ordinary/usual Pic 1

Ordinary/usual Pic 2

177

Wonderful   Pic 1

Wonderful   Pic 2

Stupid (thing)   Pic 1

Stupid (thing)   Pic 2

Sensitive   Pic 1

Sensitive   Pic 2

178

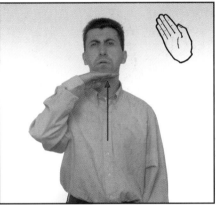

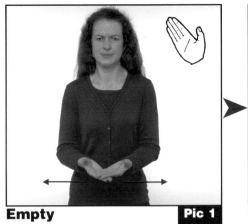

Empty Pic 1

Empty Pic 2

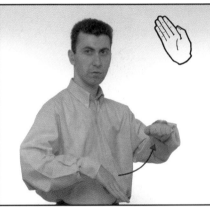

Full (no more space)

Full (of food)

Must

Spoil

179

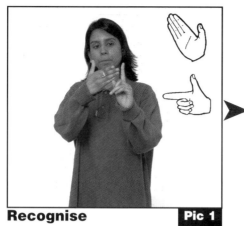

Recognise | Pic 1

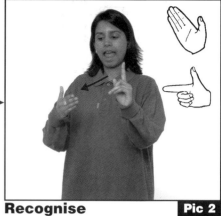

Recognise | Pic 2

Not allowed/ forbidden | Pic 1

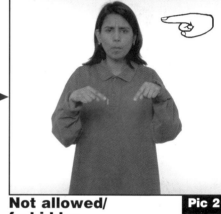

Not allowed/ forbidden | Pic 2

Allowed | Pic 1

Allowed | Pic 2

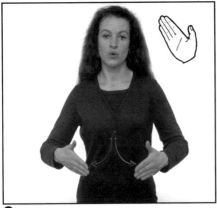

Open

Think

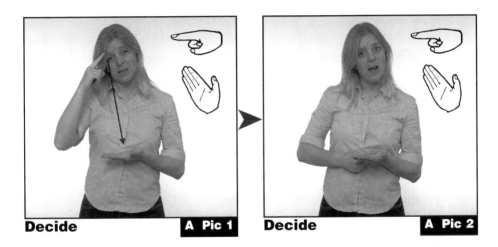

Decide   A Pic 1

Decide   A Pic 2

Decide   B Pic 1

Decide   B Pic 2

181

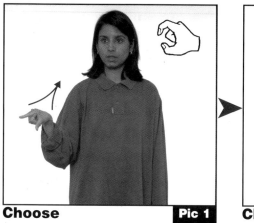

Choose — Pic 1

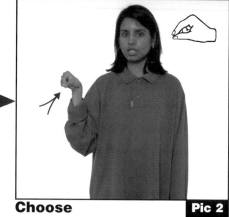

Choose — Pic 2

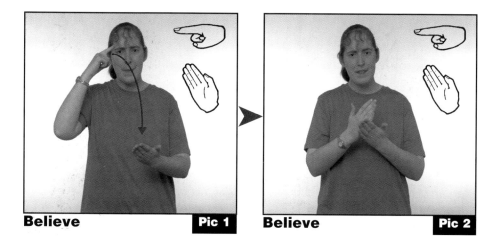

Believe — Pic 1   **Believe** — Pic 2

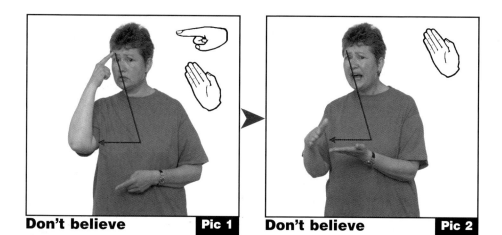

Don't believe — Pic 1   **Don't believe** — Pic 2

I know   **Pic 1**

I know   **Pic 2**

I don't know   **Pic 1**

I don't know   **Pic 2**

Ignore/avoid   **Pic 1**

Ignore/avoid   **Pic 2**

Describing and discussing

183

Defend

Doubt

Influence

Interrupt

Argue Pic 1

Argue Pic 2

Say **Pic 1**   Say **Pic 2**

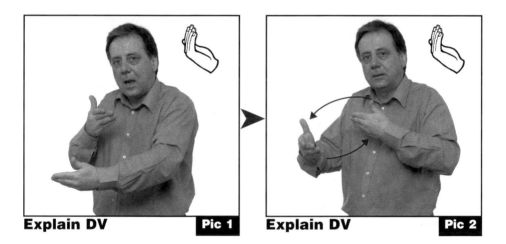

Explain DV **Pic 1**   Explain DV **Pic 2**

Opposite **Pic 1**   Opposite **Pic 2**

Can — Pic 1

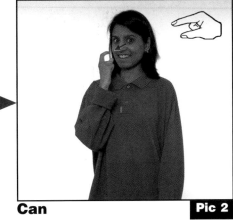

Can — Pic 2

Cannot

Compare

Won't — Pic 1

Won't — Pic 2

Will

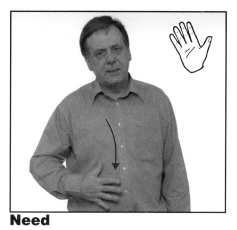

Need

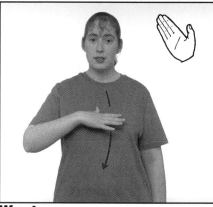

Want

Quick

Slow   Pic 1   **Slow**   Pic 2

187

Continue — Pic 1

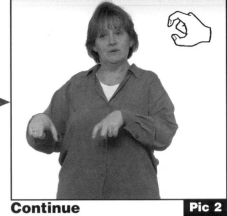

Continue — Pic 2

About (subject)

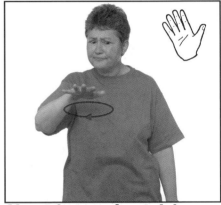

About (approximately)

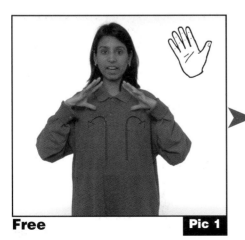

Free — Pic 1

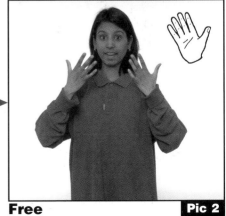

Free — Pic 2

Change

Guess

| Attitude | Pic 1 | Attitude | Pic 2 |

| Without | Pic 1 | Without | Pic 2 |

189

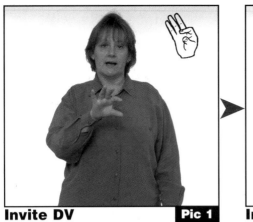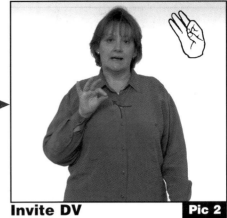

Invite DV   Pic 1   **Invite DV**   Pic 2

Together   Pic 1   **Together**   Pic 2

Discuss/talk   Pic 1   **Discuss/talk**   Pic 2

Seems

Attack/enemy

Criticise DV

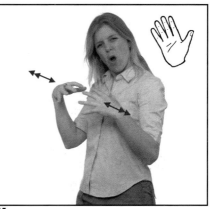

War

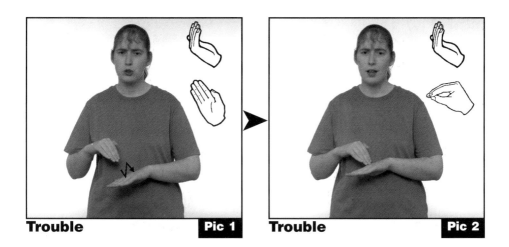

Trouble Pic 1

Trouble Pic 2

191

Young

Old

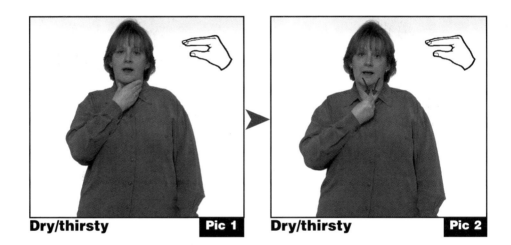

Dry/thirsty Pic 1

Dry/thirsty Pic 2

Soft

Light (weight)

Deep   Pic 1

Deep   Pic 2

Near

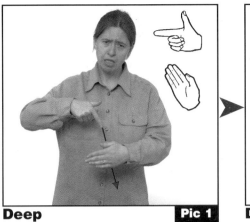

Prefer

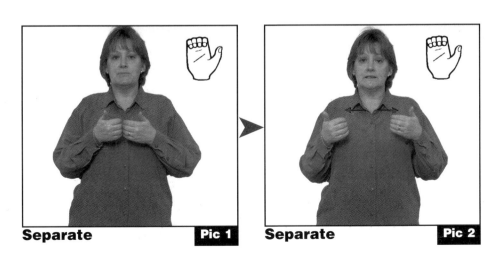

Separate   Pic 1

Separate   Pic 2

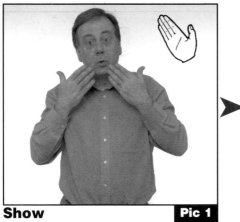

Show | Pic 1

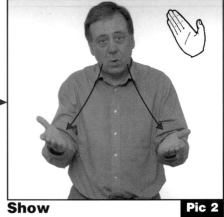

Show | Pic 2

Happen | Pic 1

Happen | Pic 2

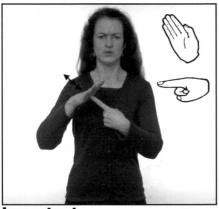

Important

Thing

Nearly

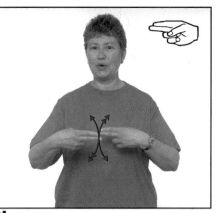

News

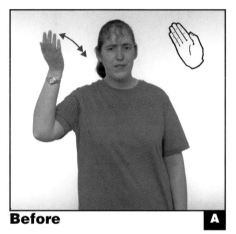

Before **A**

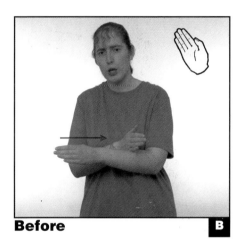

Before **B**

After

Centre

195

Long ago   `Pic 1`

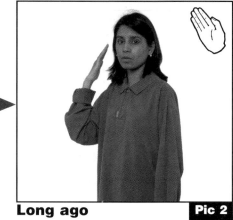

Long ago   `Pic 2`

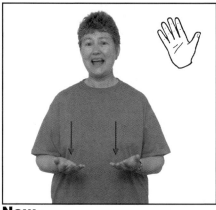

Now

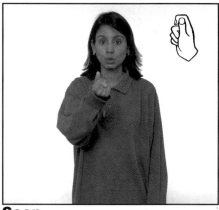

Soon

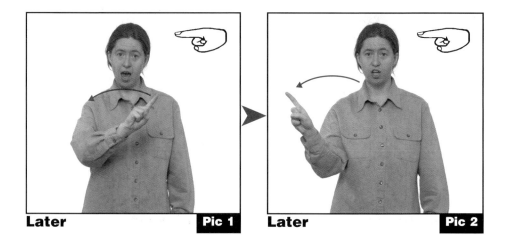

Later   `Pic 1`

Later   `Pic 2`

196

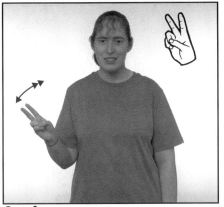

Again

Often

Sometimes | Pic 1

Sometimes | Pic 2

Regular/usually | Pic 1

Regular/usually | Pic 2

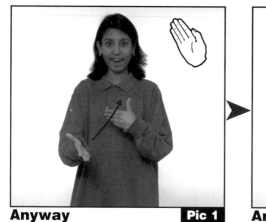

Anyway   Pic 1

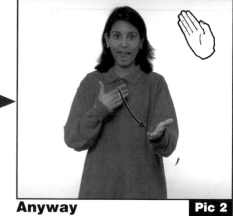

Anyway   Pic 2

Just/recently

Maybe

Possibly   Pic 1

Possibly   Pic 2

Always Pic 1   **Always** Pic 2

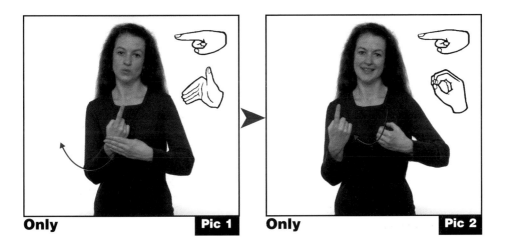

Only Pic 1   **Only** Pic 2

Enough

Both/double

Most   Pic 1   **Most**   Pic 2

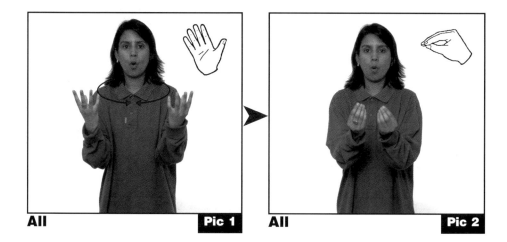

All   Pic 1   **All**   Pic 2

More (extra)

For/in favour of

Positive

Negative

With

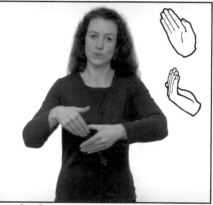

Include

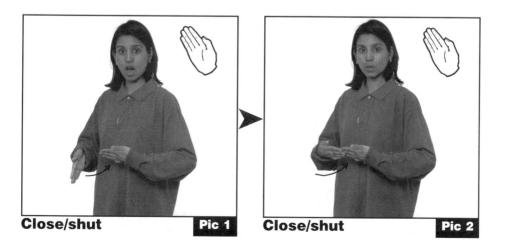

Close/shut `Pic 1`

Close/shut `Pic 2`

Light (daylight) — Pic 1

Light (daylight) — Pic 2

Stop — Pic 1

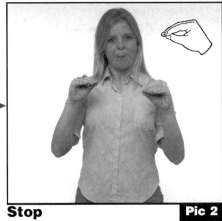

Stop — Pic 2

Fingerspelling alphabet

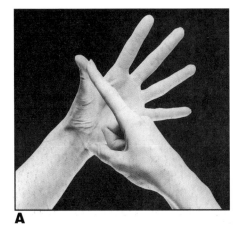

A

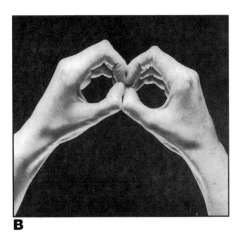

B

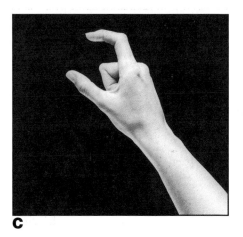

C

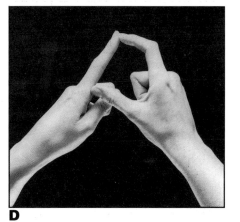

D

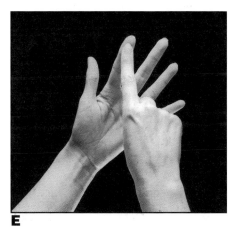

E

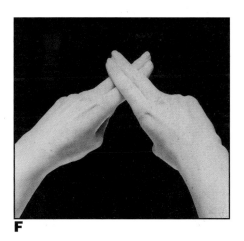

F

G

H

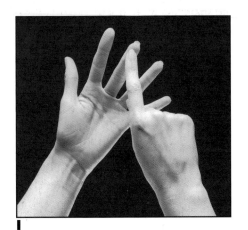

I

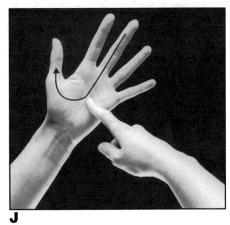

J

K

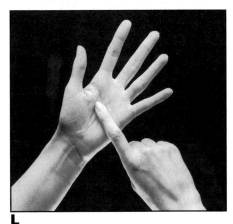

L

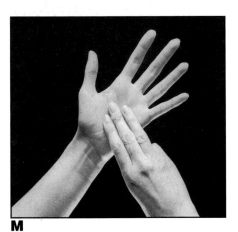

M

N

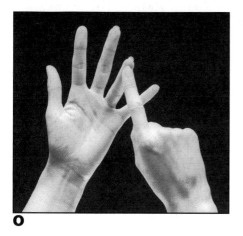

O

P

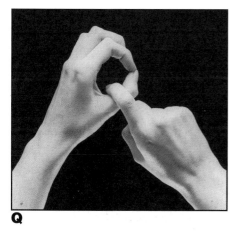

Q

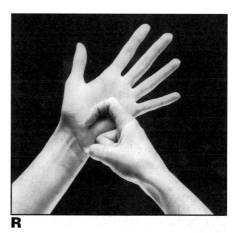

R

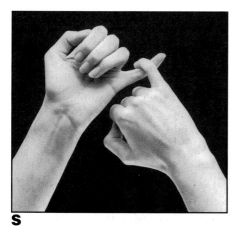

S

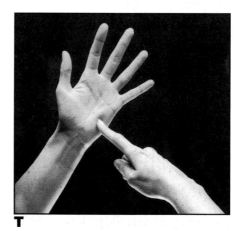

T

205

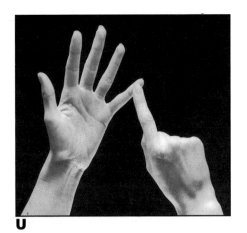

U

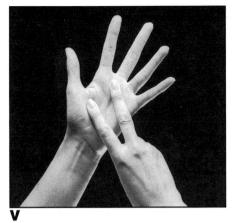

V

W

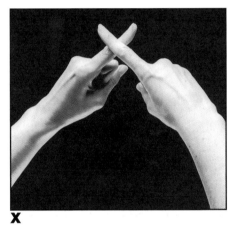

X

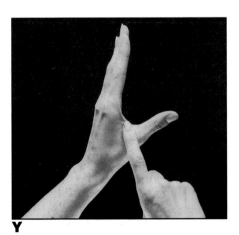

Y

Z

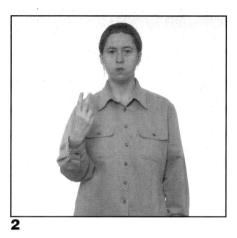

1

2

3

4

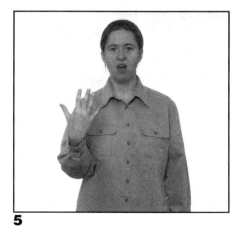

5

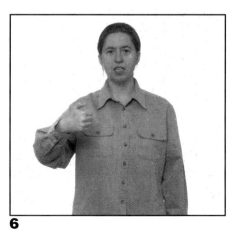

6

7

8

9

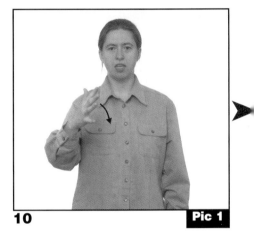

10 `Pic 1`

10 `Pic 2`

11

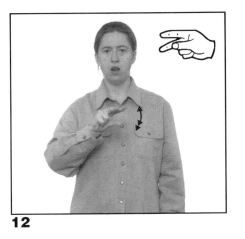

12

13

Use the fingers for 4, 5, 6, 7, 8 and 9 with this hand movement for numbers 14 to 19.

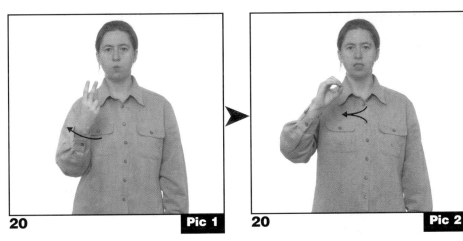

20 — Pic 1

20 — Pic 2

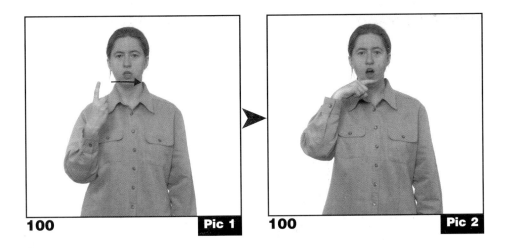

100 — Pic 1

100 — Pic 2

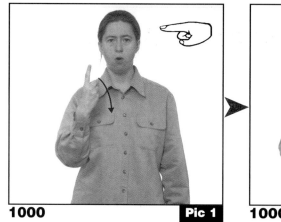

1000   **Pic 1**

1000   **Pic 2**

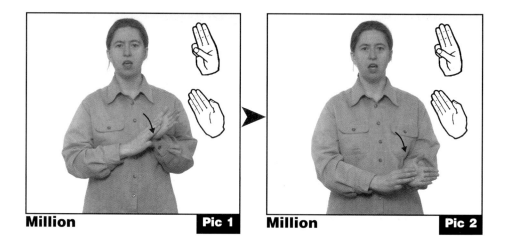

Million   **Pic 1**

Million   **Pic 2**

210

Useful organisations

If you are interested in finding out more about BSL, these organisations can help:

RNID
19-23 Featherstone Street, London EC1Y 8SL
Tel 0808 808 0123 Textphone 0808 808 9000
Fax 020 7296 8199
informationline@rnid.org.uk
www.rnid.org.uk

RNID has information on most subjects related to deafness and hearing loss. Contact us for a copy of our free publications catalogue. We can also supply details of BSL courses in your area.

British Deaf Association (BDA)
1-3 Worship Street, London EC2A 2AB
Tel 0870 770 3300 Textphone 0800 6522 965
Videophone 020 7496 9539
Fax 020 7588 3527
helpline@bda.org.uk
www.britishdeafassociation.org.uk

The BDA aims to advance the interests of the Deaf Community and promote greater awareness of their rights and responsibilities. It believes that Deaf people should be enabled, through equal access, to take their full place as members of the wider national community. It provides information and advice, organises conferences, under-takes research and campaigns on issues affecting Deaf people.

Useful organisations

Council for the Advancement of Communication with Deaf People (CACDP)
Durham University Science Park
Block 4, Stockton Road
Durham DH1 3UZ
Tel 0191 383 1155   Textphone 0191 383 7915
Fax 0191 383 7914
durham@cacdp.org.uk
www.cacdp.org.uk

CACDP is the national examining board for communication skills (British Sign Language, Lipspeaking, Deaf Awareness and Deafblind Communication) with deaf people and produces curricula and videos to help students on their courses.

Forest Books
Forest Bookshop Warehouse, New Building, Ellwood Road, Milkwall, Colford, Gloucestershire GL16 7LE
Tel 01594 833858 Textphone 01594 833507
Videophone 01594 810637
Fax 01594 833446
forest@forestbooks.com
www.forestbooks.com

Forest Books specialises in books, videos and CD-ROMs on deafness and deaf issues, keeping over 1,200 titles in stock. They have a fast and efficient mail order service, a free catalogue and a web shopping site.

Index of English meanings

E

F

film	87		G	
fine (money)	127			
finish	158		gale	126
fire	150		Gallaudet University	115
firefighter	150		garden	58
first	100		gas	68
fish	23		gay	108
fish (to eat)	46		Germany	38
flashing light	144		girl	109
flat	64		glass	44
flower	58		go	122
flu	54		go home	58
fog	126		go to sleep	62
follow	74		goal	85
football	85		gold	29
for	200		golf	83
forbidden	180		good	169
foreign	120		goodbye	83
forest	77		Government	110
forget	113		grandfather	104
forgive	162		grandmother	103
fork	44		Greece	39
fortnight	134		green	28
France	38		grow up	109
free	188		guess	189
Friday	133		guide	74
friend	108		guilty	129
from	122			
fruit	47			
frustrated	163		H	
full (no more space)	179			
full (of food)	179		half	100
funny	165		hall	67
future	137		happen	194
			happy	162
			hard	156
			hard of hearing	33
			hat	29
			hate	161

I

J

start to sign CD ROM

The ideal resource to compliment *Start to sign!*

- Over 850 colour video sign clips
- Animated fingerspelling
- Interactive quiz to check your progress
- Useful information on sign language and deafness

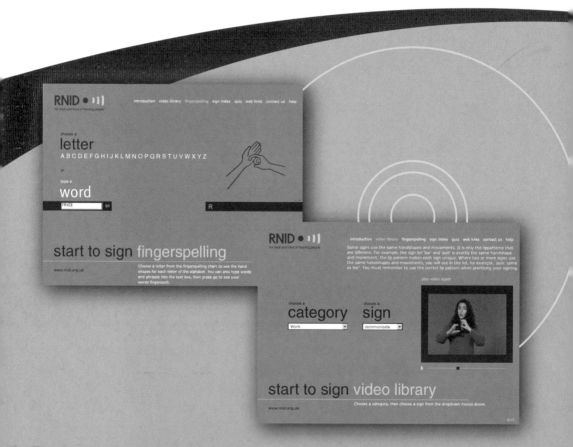

To order your copy contact the RNID Information Line:

Tel 0808 808 0123 Textphone 0808 808 9000

Fax 020 7296 8199 informationline@rnid.org.uk

www.rnidshop.com

Available to buy online www.rnidshop.com

Notes

Notes

Notes

Notes